DEFENDING

THE

GOSPEL

Kel Richards

Guidebooks for Life 👫

Bible-based essentials
for your Christian journey

Defending the Gospel is part of a series of
straightforward, practical Christian books from
Matthias Media which deal with the important nuts-
and-bolts topics that Christians need to know about as
we walk each day with our Master.

Some Christian books are all theory and no practical
application; others are all stories and tips with
no substance. The Guidebooks for Life aim to achieve
a vital balance—that is, to dig into the Bible and
discover what God is telling us there, as well
as applying that truth to our daily Christian lives.

For up-to-date information about the latest
Guidebooks for Life, visit our website:
www.matthiasmedia.com.au

GUIDEBOOKS FOR LIFE

DEFENDING

THE

GOSPEL

WHAT TO SAY
WHEN PEOPLE CHALLENGE
YOUR FAITH

matthiasmedia

Defending the Gospel
© Beacon Communications 2006

Matthias Media
(St Matthias Press Ltd. ACN 067 558 365)
PO Box 225
Kingsford NSW 2032 Australia
Telephone: (02) 9663 1478; international: +61-2-9663-1478
Facsimile: (02) 9663 3265; international: +61-2-9663-3265
Email: info@matthiasmedia.com.au
Internet: www.matthiasmedia.com.au

Matthias Media (USA)
Telephone: 724 964 8152; international: +1-724-964-8152
Facsimile: 724 964 8166; international: +1-724-964-8166
Email: sales@matthiasmedia.com
Internet: www.matthiasmedia.com

ISBN 978 1 921068 46 1

Cover design and typesetting by Lankshear Design Pty Ltd.

Printed in Singapore.

CONTENTS

Chapter 1

DEFENDING, ANSWERING AND GIVING REASONS

IT CAN BE A VERY TENSE MOMENT. It can involve looking down at your feet and shuffling your shoes. It can involve opening and shutting your mouth like a goldfish in a bowl.

It's that moment when a friend or relative or colleague asks a question or makes a comment about your Christian faith—and you realize that you haven't the faintest idea what to say in response. You have no answer. You have no reasons or reasoning to offer.

Your mind has gone blank. Your mouth has gone dry.

I remember the first time it happened to me. I was a very young radio announcer, probably all of 19, at a country station. Standing in the record library of the local radio station in Armidale, in northern New South Wales,

I heard the other young announcer beside me say, "Religion is just for people who need a crutch".

And he said it with all the wisdom and certainty of a 19-year-old (we were about the same age). He was most likely repeating a remark he had heard somewhere. But I had never come across that sort of comment before. It floored me for a moment. And then I thought of how to reply.

"No it's not!" was my intellectually and theologically powerful response.

And that was the end of the conversation.

I did badly because I hadn't done my homework. I wasn't prepared.

How would I deal with such a comment today? I guess I might say, "Well, it's a good thing that Christianity's not a religion then, isn't it?" That's a sufficiently provocative statement to get a conversation going. Later in this book, I'll explain the thinking behind that response—and how it can be useful.

If I was talking to someone a little older, with a little more experience of life, I might respond by saying, "As we get older we all discover that we need support in life, don't we? And when it comes to support, belief is better than booze. But only if it's belief in the truth, of course. That's probably why Jesus said that believing in him was like standing on solid rock."

And that might get a useful conversation going.

But at the age of 19, I completely blew it. I had no idea what I was supposed to be defending, or how, or why, or … well, anything at all about my responsibility when an unbeliever raised a faith issue.

So that's where we need to begin in this book—answering those basic **who**, **what**, **when**, **why** and **how** questions. A good place to start looking for information on all those things is in 1 Peter 3:15-16:

> ... but in your hearts regard Christ the Lord as holy, always being prepared to make a defence to anyone who asks you for a reason for the hope that is in you; yet do it with gentleness and respect ...

The context for this statement about 'making a defence' is as follows:

Peter is writing to a bunch of Christians scattered through several places in what is now Turkey. He is writing because they are either now experiencing persecution, or are about to. 1 Peter is a short letter, and it would be a good idea for you to sit down and read it right through now. It won't take long, and you'll see Peter's argument in context. One of his main reasons for writing is to tell them how to cope with persecution.

Peter's advice is: be godly—then, at least, you'll be persecuted for the right reason, not the wrong reason.

> Now who is there to harm you if you are zealous for what is good? But even if you should suffer for righteousness' sake, you will be blessed. Have no fear of them, nor be troubled ... (1 Pet 3:13-14)

Peter's statement about 'making a defence' comes in this context of what he says about living a godly life. In other words, defending the gospel is just a regular part of ordinary godliness (not that godliness is ever ordinary—but you catch my drift).

Your response might be: if ever I find myself facing persecution, I'll bear that in mind. It is easy to make the assumption that while there are places where Christians are still being persecuted for the sake of Jesus Christ, it is not happening in Western nations (such as Australia, Britain and the United States). Don't be so sure.

Persecution is not limited to physical torture. For instance, in the Gospel accounts of the crucifixion of Jesus, his terrible physical suffering is referred to, but is not described in detail or lingered over. What **is** described in detail is the shame, humiliation and mockery Jesus had to suffer.

You could be forgiven for thinking that the Gospels treat shame, humiliation and mockery as a more significant persecution than torture.

This was certainly a component in the persecution being faced by the first readers of Peter's letter: "If you are insulted for the name of Christ, you are blessed, because the Spirit of glory and of God rests upon you" (1 Pet 4:14). So being insulted was one type of persecution Peter's readers were facing. And so are we.

Christians in Western nations may (at the moment) not be facing imprisonment and torture for their beliefs. But they are certainly facing humiliation and mockery. Just think of the way the word 'fundamentalist' is used in the media these days, and you'll see what I mean. It's employed as a term of abuse designed to embarrass anyone who reads their Bible and takes it seriously.

The Da Vinci Code[1] is persecution (in this sense of the word), designed to humiliate, mock and insult Christians. In many homes and workplaces, Christians face being insulted for the gospel of Jesus Christ.

That's quite enough persecution to be going on with —and that's quite enough reason to learn the lessons Peter is teaching and put them to work in our lives.

In that context, Peter's statement in 1 Peter 3:15-16 is a command. There are lots of commands in the Bible. Some are broad in their scope, and some are narrow. Some, for instance, apply only to husbands, or only to wives, or only to parents, or only to elders. Other commands are universal, and apply to everyone. Peter's command is universal.

This statement by Peter is a general command as broad in its application as "Love your neighbour as yourself". This command applies to all Christians. It applies to you. No-one is off the hook.

So who should be making this defence? **Every** Christian.

And what is it a command to do? It's a command, first and foremost, to be prepared.

Sure, we are then commanded to use our preparation in a particular way (by making a defence). But step one in this command is: be prepared. In other words, this is a command to do your homework. Every Christian (without exception) is commanded in these words to do the preparation (the homework) that will equip them to "make a defence". Have you been doing your homework?

---

[1]   Dan Brown, *The Da Vinci Code*, Transworld Publishers, London, 2003.

If you haven't, you've been disobeying God.

Who are we meant to "make a defence" to? To "anyone who asks you for a reason for the hope that is in you". You are commanded to have reasons ready to give to anyone who asks.

There are two ways in which people can ask. They can use a straightforward question, or they can use a statement.

If someone poses the question, "Why would the God who made the universe be interested in me—one person, on one small planet, in a vast universe?", they are asking you for "a reason for the hope that is in you". But if someone makes the statement (perhaps even in a sneering, mocking tone), "The God who made the universe couldn't possibly be interested in me—one person, on one small planet, in a vast universe", they are asking you exactly the same thing. They, too, are effectively asking for "a reason for the hope that is in you". They want you to respond.

We need to learn to hear the 'asking' that comes in statements, as well as the 'asking' that comes in questions. But there's little point in us being tuned in and hearing the asking going on around us unless we have first done our homework and are prepared to give reasons and answers. This little book contains the sort of homework—the sort of preparation—we are to do.

Peter's command tells us how to give these reasons and answers. We are to answer "with gentleness and respect". The goal is not to win the argument, but to win the person. Making a defence is not playing an intellectual game. It's trying to lower the barriers and remove the obstacles, so that someone can see the good news of Jesus Christ clearly.

What is it we are meant to defend? It is "the hope that is in you". This little phrase is a way of referring to the gospel. Right at the beginning of his letter Peter had written, "Blessed be the God and Father of our Lord Jesus Christ! According to his great mercy, he has caused us to be born again to a living hope through the resurrection of Jesus Christ from the dead ..." (1 Pet 1:3). That "living hope" is what Jesus Christ has won for us by his crucifixion and resurrection. It is the "living hope" of eternal life. It is "the hope that is in you"—a phrase that Peter employs to refer to the gospel.

So then, what we are meant to defend is: the gospel.

The good news is: that means there's lots of stuff we don't have to defend.

We don't have to defend the Spanish Inquisition or the Crusades. We don't have to defend any denomination. We don't have to be defensive about the pronouncements of the Pope, the wealth of the Vatican, or cheesy televangelists. We don't have to defend the foreign policy of any so-called 'Christian nation'. We don't have to defend the behaviour of an abusive churchgoing parent or an insensitive Sunday School teacher. We don't have to defend the false assumptions people may have about Christianity. We don't have to defend 'religion'.

We choose the ground on which we stand and make a defence. Or, rather, the Bible has chosen the ground for us: we are to defend **the gospel**.

Why should we do this? Because doing this is part of "in your hearts regard[ing] Christ the Lord as holy".

Doing this homework; being sensitive enough to hear when people are 'asking'; then responding with reasons and answers, and doing so with gentleness and respect—all this is part of honouring Christ. Failing to do that is failing to honour Christ.

Paul expresses much the same command in a slightly different way in Colossians 4:5-6 when he writes:

> Conduct yourselves wisely towards outsiders, making the best use of the time. Let your speech always be gracious, seasoned with salt, so that you may know how you ought to answer each person.

Once again this is a general command, applicable to all Christians, about how they are to behave towards unbelievers. As expressed by Paul, this instruction has several components.

Firstly, our conduct is on view here. We are to conduct ourselves wisely towards outsiders. We are to conduct ourselves like followers of Jesus Christ. We are to live Christianly. We are to live godly lives—lives that just might lead people around us to ask about the master we serve, and will certainly help to recommend any answers we give.

Secondly, our time belongs to Jesus. We are to make the best use of it we can. If we have a choice between discussing the weather (or the football, or last night's television) or picking up on the 'asking' someone has done with a question or statement, we are to do the latter. We are to choose to use the time well by answering them, and defending the gospel.

Thirdly, our speech is to be "gracious". This is Peter's

notion of "gentleness and respect" expressed in another word. We are not to be smart alecs who have pat answers for everything, but people who are genuinely interested in unbelievers and who want to graciously help them see the gospel.

Fourthly, our talk is to be "seasoned with salt". This salt image appears elsewhere in Scripture—for instance, in the Sermon on the Mount when Jesus says, "You are the salt of the earth, but if salt has lost its taste, how shall its saltiness be restored? It is no longer good for anything except to be thrown out and trampled under people's feet" (Matt 5:13).

The point of this salt image seems to be that salt is unlike whatever it's added to. It is the difference between the salt and what it's added to that makes salt worthwhile. If salt loses its difference, it becomes useless.

In other words, if our lives and our conversation become exactly like the lives and conversations of the unbelievers around us then we are useless. Our role, in whatever situation we find ourselves, is to be different. This, of course, invites mockery, insults and humiliation—but that goes with the territory of following Jesus. We are to be different nonetheless, or else we become a waste of oxygen.

Fifthly, we are to "know how ... to answer each person". This is that familiar instruction to be prepared (to do our homework) expressed in slightly different words.

These two statements from Peter and Paul record a command from God that works out as being a series of steps:

1. Do your homework (be prepared).
2. As a result, know how to reason and answer.
3. Live Christianly, so that if people around you have questions or comments about Christianity, you'll be the person they ask.
4. Listen attentively for the various ways in which people 'ask' (with statements as well as questions).
5. Give your reasons and answers gently, graciously and respectfully.

If we do these things then we are obeying this universal command that God's word imposes on all Christians (and we are honouring Jesus Christ as Lord).

There are two other things that need to be stressed if we are to be obedient to this command. The first is: pray, pray, pray. The second is: listen, listen, listen.

Prayer is essential. We don't do any gospel work on our own, even if we are the only Christian in our particular home, classroom or office. Jesus goes with us, and he even goes before us, speaking to the hearts and minds of unbelievers. Indeed, Jesus is the real evangelist. We just tag along behind, answering the questions provoked by his work in hearts and minds.

You're more likely to pick up on a subtle bit of 'asking' from a friend or colleague if you've been praying for that person. Nothing makes you more tuned in to a person's interest than praying for them.

And we need to be praying for ourselves as well as others. We need to pray that the right bit of our preparation (our homework) pops into our head at the right time. And we need to pray that we'll find the right words to explain our reasons and answers clearly.

Then we need to listen. It is very easy to hear a question, or an objection, and want to leap right in because you are sure that you know the answer to it. Don't. Much better to draw a deep breath and say, "What do you mean by that?" Let people you are responding to explain themselves. It may be that what really troubles them is not quite what you had first assumed it to be. As they go on speaking, you will start to understand what really troubles them and what you really need to be answering.

Furthermore, we earn the right to speak by being willing to listen. If we will give them time, and listen patiently and sympathetically, then they are more likely to listen to us when we offer reasons and answers. Of course, they may not. There are no guarantees. Just because you've earned the right to a hearing doesn't mean you'll always get one. But listening carefully, closely, and at some length is still the best step to take before reasoning and answering.

By praying, and listening, and going through those five steps that are part of obeying this command, we will be acknowledging our Lord and saviour, our ruler and rescuer, Jesus Christ, who said, "Everyone who acknowledges me before men, I also will acknowledge before my Father who is in heaven" (Matt 10:32).

The other side of this coin is that silence is denial. To fail to answer when we're asked amounts to denying our Lord. "Whoever denies me before men, I also will deny before my Father who is in heaven" (Matt 10:33). To respond to someone's asking by giving a blank look that implies, "Don't ask me—I wouldn't know, and, anyway, I don't want to talk about it" is to deny Jesus.

In seeing that what we need to defend is the gospel, and not a lot of extraneous stuff, there is one more point to be made: the gospel is the logic of the universe. The gospel has a built-in persuasive power of its own. The gospel is coherent, consistent and logical.

The gospel has 'explanatory power'—it makes sense of the world around us; it explains why the world is the way it is; it explains God's purpose for us in the world; it explains who Jesus is, why he came, and what he requires of us.

Of course, there are plenty of unbelievers who will remain unbelievers even after the gospel has been explained and defended. But those people God changes, he changes using the gospel: "I am not ashamed of the gospel, for it is the power of God for salvation to everyone who believes ..." (Rom 1:16). It is the gospel itself that is "the power of God", not the cleverness of our answers or reasons.

That takes a great weight off our shoulders. We don't need to be persuasive—we need to be clear. We need to give honest, biblical reasons and answers, and leave the rest to the power of God—the gospel.

So the answer to the question, "What are Christians to defend?" is: "The gospel". That means that step one in doing our preparation is to learn the gospel.

There are a number of helpful gospel outlines available, however, this guidebook is going to use the

Two Ways to Live [2] gospel outline. There are two reasons why I've chosen to use this gospel outline (rather than one of the others).

First, I'm writing this book so I get to pick. Second, *Two Ways to Live* is a comprehensive gospel outline that sets the gospel of Jesus Christ crucified and risen into the context of the biblical world view. And that's powerful in an age in which so many people don't understand (or confidently misunderstand) the Bible's world view.

If you prefer another gospel outline, I'm certain you'll find that the material in the following chapters can be fitted into whichever outline you prefer.

Two Ways to Live covers the gospel in six points. If you haven't come across *Two Ways to Live* before then it may be that as well as learning ways to reason and answer in defence of the gospel, you'll also learn a useful gospel outline.

Those, then, are the answers to the basic **who**, **what**, **why** and **how** questions. All that is left is the **when** question.

And the answer to **when** is **now** and **always**: now is the time to be doing your homework; and you should always be ready to respond (always ready to answer, defend and give reasons).

---

[2]   Phillip D. Jensen and Tony Payne, *Two ways to live: the choice we all face*, Matthias Media, Sydney, 2003.

IN SUMMARY:

- Do your preparation
- Know how to answer
- Live Christianly
- Pray often
- Listen carefully
- Answer graciously

Two Ways to Live:
an outline of the gospel[3]

1 | God is the loving maker and ruler of the world

God is the loving ruler of the world.

He made the world.

He made us rulers of the world under him.

The Bible says:

> *You are worthy, our Lord and God, to receive glory and honour and power, for you created all things, and by your will they were created and have their being.*

> REVELATION CHAPTER 4, VERSE II

But is that the way it is now?

---

[3]   Bible verses in this gospel outline are from the New International Version (NIV).

2 | Humanity is in rebellion

We all reject the ruler—God—by trying to run life our own way without him.

But we fail to rule ourselves or society or the world.

The Bible says:

There is no-one righteous, not even one; there is no-one who understands, no-one who seeks God. All have turned away.

ROMANS CHAPTER 3, VERSES 10-12

What will God do about this rebellion?

3 | God won't let people go on rebelling forever

God won't let us rebel forever.

God's punishment for rebellion is death and judgement.

The Bible says:

> *Man is destined to die once, and after that to face judgement.*
>
> <small>HEBREWS CHAPTER 9, VERSE 27</small>

God's justice sounds hard. But ...

4 | Jesus is the man who dies for rebels

Because of his love, God sent his Son into the world: the man Jesus Christ.

Jesus always lived under God's rule.

Yet by dying in our place he took our punishment and brought forgiveness.

The Bible says:

Christ died for sins once for all, the righteous for the unrighteous, to bring you to God.

1 PETER CHAPTER 3, VERSE 18

But that's not all ...

5 | Jesus is the risen ruler

God raised Jesus to life again as the ruler of the world.

Jesus has conquered death, now gives new life, and will return to judge.

The Bible says:

In his great mercy he has given us new birth into a living hope through the resurrection of Jesus Christ from the dead.

1 PETER CHAPTER 1, VERSE 3

Well, where does that leave us?

6 | The two ways to live

A. OUR WAY:

- Reject the ruler—God
- Try to run life our own way

Result:

- Condemned by God
- Facing death and judgement

B. GOD'S NEW WAY:

- Submit to Jesus as our ruler
- Rely on Jesus' death and resurrection

Result:

- Forgiven by God
- Given eternal life

The Bible says:

Whoever believes in the Son has eternal life, but whoever rejects the Son will not see life, for God's wrath remains on him.

JOHN CHAPTER 3, VERSE 36

Which of these represents the way you want to live?

Chapter 2

DEFENDING GOD

What the gospel says

The first point of the gospel message is that God is in charge of the world. He is the ruler, the supreme president, the king. Unlike human rulers, however, God always does what is best for his subjects. He is the kind of king you'd like to be ruled by.

God rules the world because he made the world. Like a potter with his clay, God fashioned the world into just the shape he wished, with all its amazing details. He made it, and he owns it.

He also made us. God created people who were something like himself, and put them in charge of the world—to rule it, to care for it, to be responsible for it, and to enjoy all its beauty and goodness. He appointed humanity to supervise and look after the world, but always under his own authority, honouring him and obeying his directions.

As the Bible puts it:

You are worthy, our Lord and God, to receive glory
and honour and power, for you created all things, and
by your will they were created and have their being.
(Rev 4:11, NIV)

W HAT QUESTIONS OR CHALLENGES are you likely to hear
on this first point of the gospel?

It is actually very rare to hear someone deny the existence of God. Yes, I know it does happen—but it is rare.
True atheism is not common. The Atheist Society could
hold its annual general meeting in the cupboard under
the stairs. It's not a big group.

The reason why atheism is such an unpopular hobby
is explained for us by the Bible in what could be called,
if we wanted to give it a name, 'The Common Sense
Argument from Creation'. Here it is:

For the wrath of God is revealed from heaven against
all ungodliness and unrighteousness of men, who by
their unrighteousness suppress the truth. For what
can be known about God is plain to them, because
God has shown it to them. For his invisible attributes,
namely, his eternal power and divine nature, have
been clearly perceived, ever since the creation of the
world, in the things that have been made. So they are
without excuse. (Rom 1:18-20)

In effect, this argument is saying that no argument is needed. When you just **look** at creation it should tell you that its creator is, firstly, God (has a "divine nature") and, secondly, powerful (has "eternal power"). That's what you see in a spectacular thunderstorm, a night sky filled with stars, or a blue sky piled high with a mountain of clouds.

And what Paul says, history confirms as true for the vast majority of people who have lived, or currently live, on Planet Earth. Belief in God (in one form or another) is common; unbelief is rare.

Even the famous atheist Richard Dawkins agrees that the world around us **looks** as if it is the product of creation: "The complexity of living organisms is matched by the elegant efficiency of their apparent design."[1]

We can understand 'The Common Sense Argument from Creation' Paul is using here if we see clearly the difference between what is produced by accident and what is produced by creation.

Imagine a modern painter who first blindfolds himself, and then flings pots of paint at a canvas. The resulting 'work of art' is not the product of creation. It has been made by chance and by accident. It tells us nothing about its maker. It even leaves us unsure that it had a maker at all—was it the result of an explosion in a paint factory? By way of contrast, a portrait by Rembrandt

---

[1]   Richard Dawkins, *The Blind Watchmaker: Why the Evidence of Evolution Reveals a Universe Without Design,* reissued edn, W.W. Norton, New York, 1996 (1986), p. xiii.

is a product of creation. Rembrandt portraits don't happen by accident (by blindfolded paint-throwing).

Well, what does the world around us most resemble: a Rembrandt portrait or an explosion in a paint factory? Most people say the portrait not the paint explosion. That's why most people believe in the existence of a creator who is both God and also eternally powerful. It's straightforward common sense. And it's what the Bible is talking about when it points us to what can be "clearly perceived" in "the things that have been made".

However, what Paul is mainly doing in this passage is helping us to understand why, when the existence of God is as obvious as a flashing neon sign, some people still want to argue the toss, or refuse to live with God as their God. Why do they still ignore him and rebel against him? Unbelievers are actually, Paul tells us, working hard, using their intellects to "suppress the truth"—to suppress the message that creation is constantly pumping out at them. And by doing this 'suppressing' they are being 'ungodly' and 'unrighteous'. What they are displaying are the effects of sin—which we'll read about in the next chapter.

In the meantime, these words are an encouragement not to argue for what doesn't need arguing for. Talk to your non-Christian friends and listen to them; if they believe God exists, then move on from there.

Paul's words help us to understand what we most often don't need to argue for. The Bible is saying that anyone who sees creation doesn't need to have the existence of the creator—the eternally powerful God—spelled out.

Dealing with a minority sidetrack

But what about the minority? What about the person who actually rejects the existence of God? In our modern Western world what they are most likely to say is something along the lines of, "Science has shown how this so-called 'creation' can come about by chance and accident. So I don't look at creation and say 'God'. In fact, science helps me to be quite comfortable in believing that there is no such thing as God."

This person is probably appealing to some form of evolution or Darwinism. However, they are mistaken if they think that evolutionary science disproves God. Evolution—even if it turned out to be true—is not evidence for atheism.

That obviously needs a bit of explaining, but first, a word of advice. If anyone ever opens up the whole evolution or Darwinism can of worms, don't argue the science with them. The moment you do, you are admitting that science will settle the existence of God, one way or the other. It won't. Just by being drawn into an argument about the science you are giving the game away, and unwittingly granting the atheist's (false) claim that science has authority over the Bible.

Leave arguments about the science of evolution to professional scientists. There are plenty of Christians who are professional scientists and will engage in the debate in the appropriate professional scientific forums.

For those of us who are not professional scientists, we just have to remember: science is not evidence for atheism. More specifically, evolutionary science, even if it turned out to be true, is not evidence for atheism.

The falsehood that science in general, or evolution in particular, is evidence for atheism is based on a confusion between **process** and **purpose**.

What science aims to explain, and claims to explain, is the process by which the natural world around us works and came into being. But explaining process is not the same thing as explaining purpose.

Famous atheist Richard Dawkins is typical of the confusion that results from muddling up process and purpose. In his book *The Blind Watchmaker*[2] Dawkins says that if he was asked to explain a motor car, he would do so in terms of cylinders, pistons, spark plugs and so on. In other words, he would explain the process.

However, if he was asked to explain why 'that car went through that red light', then no explanation in terms of cylinders, pistons, spark plugs and so on would do. No explanation in terms of process would answer that question. What is being sought is not the process but the purpose.

Richard Dawkins doesn't understand what it means to explain, because he thinks that all explaining means explaining processes. He seems to think that if he's explained the process then he's explained everything. But process is only half of the explanation; the other half is purpose.

---

2   ibid., p. 12.

Even if the evolutionary story turned out to be completely true, it would still only explain the **process** of life on earth. It can't explain the **purpose** of life on earth. And explaining process doesn't eliminate the possibility that there is a purpose. Just because you can explain how the paint in a Rembrandt got to be arranged on the canvas, doesn't mean you can explain Rembrandt's **purpose** in painting it in the first place.

Purpose is beyond the scope of science. Science is focused entirely on process. By way of contrast, the Bible devotes very little space to explaining the process—but instead devotes itself to explaining the purpose. The Bible focuses on who and why—not how.

The Bible tells us that God, the Mind behind the Universe, began the whole process out of nothing. But the Bible provides very little detail as to what that process was. Further down the track, the Bible tells us, God made some things out of other things that already existed (Gen 2:7 and 2:22). Again, the Bible tells us who and why, but not how.

The Bible tells us that God wrote the recipe for the universe, but it doesn't give us the detailed recipe (i.e. the processes and amounts and methods involved in cooking up an entire universe). The Bible focuses on purpose— on why, not how. The Bible contains no information on the geological age of the earth, or the astronomical age of the universe. But it does spell out, in detail, the purpose and plan God is unfolding over the ages.

In other words: don't get sidetracked. The gospel is about the purpose behind the natural world, and our role in that purpose. It's not about the processes by which the natural world operates.

If human beings have today developed (or evolved) such that we are (on average) taller than human beings were several centuries ago, that has something to do with natural selection, environmental variables and the complex information encoded in human DNA. That is part of the process. But if you want to know the purpose of human beings and the role we are meant to play in creation, you have to go to the Bible.

Science does process; the Bible does purpose.

There are, of course, people who refuse to see this. But, says the Bible, this would be one example of how people "suppress the truth" and are "without excuse". They are using scientific knowledge of processes to avoid considering the far bigger issue of purpose.

What can you do with someone like that? Pray for them, and treat them with gentleness and respect. But until they look beyond process to purpose, God's message will not become clear to them.

All of this is a bit of a side issue because, as I said, it simply doesn't arise for most people. In the course of history, genuine atheists are rare.

But does God even care?

There are other problems people may run into. For instance, some may find it hard to understand how God could be interested in them. That's the question I quoted in the introduction: "Why would the God who made the universe be interested in me—one person, on one small planet, in a vast universe?"

The real answer to that question is: "Why not?"

God is God, and God's interests must (obviously) be vastly wider than ours, and far beyond ours. We are only interested in things that get our attention or attract our interest. But we are not God. We must not assume that a mind big enough to make a universe is as limited as ours.

Furthermore, size doesn't indicate importance. If it did, a newborn baby would automatically and necessarily be less important than an elephant. A diamond engagement ring would automatically and necessarily be less important than a vacuum cleaner.

The questioner who protests that "God wouldn't be interested in me" is really claiming to know something about God. They are claiming to know what range of things God would be interested in.

Most probably they are guessing what God would be like based on what the important human beings they know are like. The big boss of the factory takes very little interest in the tea lady or the apprentice boy. God, they think, must be like that.

But we know God is not like that by looking at the world around us. The Bible tells us that God's "invisible attributes, namely, his eternal power and divine nature, have been clearly perceived ... in the things that have been made" (Rom 1:20). In other words, we get some idea about the nature of God—even what he is **not** like— from every beautiful sunrise, every glorious sunset, a flower in full bloom, a playful kitten, a newborn baby, or the sound of birdsong outside the window.

Whoever made these things is not like the Managing Director of the United Widget Factory.

Human beings who are capable of love, joy, writing poetry, painting portraits and composing symphonies did not come from a God who is a cold-hearted chief accountant. If anything, the very opposite is true. What we can see in the world around us is a generous, creative interest in the details. God's eternal power and divine nature can be seen in what he has made.

Of course, there are clearly things wrong with the world. This is not a perfect planet. But the fault is found in human nature, not God's nature. That's the Bible's message. In fact, that's the second point in our gospel outline, and we'll look at it in some detail in the next chapter.

The answer to the question, "Why would God be interested in me?" is: "Because God is like that". God made human beings to be the way we are and he continues to take an interest in us because God is like that.

It is because God is like that, the Bible tells us, that God created people who were something like himself.

But aren't we just smart animals?

At this point there is another objection that is sometimes raised. Human beings, the cynic says, are just smart animals. We may have more complex brains than other animals, but we're just animals—and we're being arrogant and egotistical to think that God should be especially interested in us.

Such people are likely to say, "We share 99% of our DNA with monkeys" or something of the sort. So, they seem to imply, we are just hairless monkeys with large brains. "That", they say, "doesn't make human beings anything other than the dominant species on an animal-inhabited planet".

And that argument, they think, sinks the idea that God has put human beings here as his representatives —with a special place and purpose in his plan.

People who think like this are just not paying attention. Whatever the DNA says, the difference between humans and the great apes is not one or two per cent. It is a massive gap: a Grand-Canyon-sized gap.

It's not the case that human beings are flying jumbo jets, while the chimps are only up to simple biplanes. It's not the case that human beings are building skyscrapers, while gorillas are only up to making single-storey brick houses. It's not the case that human beings are composing symphonies, while baboons are only composing simple folk songs.

The apes are doing none of those things.

Zoologists get excited if they find chimpanzees in the wild using a stick as a 'tool' to dig honey out of a beehive. Meanwhile, human beings are making (and using) sophisticated electronic instruments.

Once again, it's a case of observation and common sense.

Observation and common sense tell us that, however cute baby chimps might be, the resemblance between them and baby humans is only superficial. The whole of the creative, built world around us has been built by humans. However clever dolphins might be at jumping through hoops, they've never built a rowing boat—let alone a nuclear-powered submarine.

This massive Grand-Canyon-sized gap between humans and even the highest animals should be shouting out to us that humans are special and, as such, have a special role and a special responsibility on this planet.

Take a look around—the one thing the human race is, is creative.

From pre-historic cave paintings by stone age man, to the artists of ancient Egypt, to the writers and sculptors of ancient Greece, to the creative energy of the Roman Empire, to the birth of modern Europe, to Shakespeare, Bach, Mozart, Beethoven, to the invention of the computer, to modern communications ... well, there's no need to go on, because the point is obvious.

It's almost as if we can't help ourselves: from the great writers, composers, scientists and inventors down to the bloke who knocks up some kitchen cupboards in his back shed, or his wife who lays out a new garden and does flower arranging.

This brings us back to the Bible's message, the gospel, which tells us that God created people who were something like himself, and put them in charge of the world.

What does 'something like himself' mean? Is there any bit of evidence still around the place that seems to hint that human beings are 'something like' God?

Well, we can know for certain that God is a creator. The creation around us points beyond itself—it points us to its creator. And if such a creative creator makes a race of people 'something like himself', what will they be? At the **very least** they too will be creative.

The weight of the evidence is that the human race is almost bubbling over with creativity. This is one small way in which we are 'something like' the creator who made the world, and then made us to resemble himself. We were made by the 'big creator' to be 'little creators' living inside his creation—and (more importantly) to manage it according to his instructions.

Creativity is undeniably a characteristic of the human race. That creativity is one small way in which we resemble the one who made us—the creator God: the loving maker and ruler of the world. And just as God's creativity can be broken down into his making and ruling of the world, so God gives us a similar role of making and ruling in his world.

So if we resemble the creator God, it's because he made us 'something like himself' **for a purpose**. This is what the Bible knows, and what science can never discover—our purpose. And that is: to be God's representatives in managing this world. Sadly, it's a job we haven't done very well (but that's point two in our gospel outline).

IN SUMMARY:
- The vast majority of people believe in God, and this has been the case throughout history.
- Observation and common sense tell us that we live in a world of beautifully complex creation—a 'made' world that points beyond itself to its maker (the

eternally powerful God).

- Science doesn't refute this obvious fact, because science looks only at process. Process tells us nothing about any purpose which might be at work in the world.
- God's interests are wider than the widest human interests. So we should not be surprised that God is interested in each individual, even though important and powerful human beings might not be.
- Observation and common sense tell us there is a vast distance between human beings and even the highest of the animals—making it clear that human beings have a special place, and a special responsibility, in God's creation.
- The human race shows its 'family resemblance' to its creator by being itself highly creative and by ruling in God's world just as he does.

Taken together, these half-a-dozen facts tell us that God is our loving maker and ruler (just as the Bible says) and that he has made us 'something like himself'—for a purpose.

Chapter 3

DEFENDING SIN

THAT'S A SLIGHTLY STARTLING chapter title, isn't it? "Defending sin" sounds a rather odd thing to do, if you are meant to be defending the gospel. However, what I mean by those two words is not defending sin as good, but defending sin as real. I'm not saying that it's good to sin, but that it's good to recognize the reality of sin. That is what the people around us may have difficulty accepting.

They shouldn't.

The one thing that should be obvious is that this is not a perfect world. There's a lot wrong with it. In fact, some people object to the existence of a loving God on the grounds that there are heaps of things wrong with the world. This is not a perfect planet. But the reason for the imperfection—for the hurt, evil and suffering we see—is found in human nature, not God's nature.

The way things should be is in harmony: human beings managing the world, in creative ways, according to God's directions. But that's clearly not the way things are. In the news every day, in home after home, in workplace after workplace, what is missing is harmony.

This planet can be a painful place to live. There is hurt and suffering. So, if a loving God made a wonderful world, what went wrong? The Bible's answer is that **we** did.

This is point two in our gospel outline.

What the gospel says

We all reject the ruler, God, by trying to run our own lives our own way without him. The sad truth is that, from the very beginning, men and women everywhere (and kids too) have rejected God by doing things their own way. We all do it.

We don't like someone telling us what to do or how to live (not even God), and so we rebel against him in lots of different ways. We ignore him and just get on with our own lives; or we disobey his instructions for living in his world; or we shake our fists in his face and tell him to get lost.

However we do it, we are all rebels, because we don't live God's way, under God's directions. We prefer to follow our own desires, and to run things our own way, without God.

This rebellious, self-sufficient attitude is what the Bible calls 'sin'. It is what lies at the core of human nature. It is what's gone wrong with the world. Sin is the human race's 'declaration of independence' against God. Instead of managing and ruling the world God's way, we've tried to rule it our own way.

And we have failed. We fail to rule ourselves or others or society or the world around us.

By ignoring God's directions we make a mess not only of our own lives, but of our society and the world. Every individual repeats our species-wide pattern of ignoring God. The result is that we end up damaging ourselves, damaging relationships, damaging other people, and damaging the creation around us.

The whole world is full of people bent on doing what suits them, and not following God's ways. We all act like little gods competing with one another over who'll be in charge. The result is misery. The suffering and injustice that we see around us all goes back to our basic rebellion against God.

That's the truth about human nature, about the human heart. The Bible says the problem is universal.

> There is no-one righteous, not even one; there is no-one who understands, no-one who seeks God. All have turned away. (Rom 3:10-12, NIV)

Jesus endorsed this view when he said:

> "For from within, out of the heart of man, come evil thoughts, sexual immorality, theft, murder, adultery, coveting, wickedness, deceit, sensuality, envy, slander, pride, foolishness." (Mark 7:21-22)

So, WHAT QUESTIONS OR CHALLENGES are you likely to hear on this second point of the gospel?

The real problem here is that this is a truth unbelievers just don't want to see. The evidence for the corruption of human nature is overwhelming—but unbelievers refuse to be overwhelmed by it. The reason is personal. If I admit that human nature is basically corrupt, that means admitting that **my** nature is corrupt. And no-one is comfortable putting up their hand and admitting "I'm basically a bad person".

That is why people become defensive. That is why people deny the evidence of their eyes, and the evidence of their own experience.

This can be a very difficult barrier to get over, so let's take it in five steps.

Step 1

The biblical definition of sin needs to be explained, to replace the world's false definition of sin. Sin is not some people breaking some of the rules some of the time. It's all people rebelling against God by ignoring him, and running their lives their own way. That commonplace of life (running your own life) is sin. It's what killed Christ; it's what needs forgiveness.

Most people think sin is defined as 'breaking the rules'. Since most people only break the rules some of the time, 'sin' (defined as 'rule-breaking') cannot, they reason, be the source of all the hurt, evil and suffering in the world.

There just isn't enough 'rule-breaking' to cause all that's wrong with the world.

Seeing 'sin' as 'rule-breaking' means people don't see sin as a basic flaw in human nature. The majority of the 'rule-breaking' they see is done by a minority of people. On this view, it's only a minority of people (the criminal classes) who break the big rules, or who make a habit of rule-breaking.

On this view most people are good, upright, law-abiding citizens who only ever break the small rules. They don't even do that very often. On this view, most people try to do the right thing, and are by and large sincere and well-meaning. The gospel's suggestion that human nature is rotten to the core is deeply offensive, and somewhat alarming.

The answer to this sort of objection is to challenge the definition of 'sin' as 'rule-breaking'. Sin certainly involves rule-breaking. But sin has to be seen as something much bigger and much more significant than that.

From the point of view of the gospel, Jesus Christ died to deal with sin. Jesus certainly didn't die because some people sometimes break some of the rules. On the cross, God died. The Son of God shed his blood to deal with sin. If that's the answer, the question must be something huge. And sin is huge—it is of cosmic proportions.

Here is a better definition of sin, that helps us to see this: 'sin' means 'running your own life without God'. It's more than just rule-breaking, although it certainly includes this. But rule-breaking is a symptom of a more serious disease. If you ask most people in the world who runs their life, who calls the shots in their life, the most common answer you will get is, "I do. I'm an adult, I'm responsible, I run my life." That's sin. That's what killed Christ. That's what ruined creation.

Picture God as the builder and landlord of a beautiful house. The landlord gave the keys of the house to the human race, and told us to manage the property according to his instructions—instead of which, we've taken over the property as if it was our own, and largely ignored his instructions. We're like bad tenants who've made a mess of a rented house. We have broken the landlord's rules, and even more than that: we've rejected the landlord's authority.

Step 2

All the wrongs in the world go back to that big basic universe-sized wrong: human beings ignoring God and running their own lives. All the other wrongs and hurts flow from this in a basic cause-and-effect relationship.

There is a direct cause-and-effect relationship between human beings running their lives in place of God, and wrongdoing. In one sense this is just logical. Anyone who respected God, and whose life was completely under the direction of God, would not rob banks, deal drugs or commit adultery.

Think of it like this. Everyone has something or someone they look to as God: themselves, something else, or—for Christians—God himself. And if I am 'god' in my life, and you are 'god' in your life, then who will be 'god' when we meet? Almost certainly, we won't agree on that. That's why relationships break down and tensions develop. That's why so many human relationships are like diplomatic negotiations between hostile nations. That's the source of the wrongdoing, the hurt, the evil, the suffering in the world.

Jesus linked these two principles together when he summarized God's requirements in just two commandments:

> "And you shall love the Lord your God with all your heart and with all your soul and with all your mind and with all your strength ... [and] you shall love your neighbour as yourself." (Mark 12:30-31)

The first is the source of the second. The person who fails to love God with all their heart, soul, mind and strength is unable to love their neighbour as themselves. We do the wrong thing. We fail to do the right thing. We do wrong, or fail, because we reject God's rule: we are not in relationship with him.

If a person is unplugged from God ('running their own life' in place of God) then they are unplugged from the source of the power that keeps them on the moral track—and wrongdoing follows as surely as night follows day.

Step 3

Those small wrongs are evidence of the big wrong—rebellion against God—that lies behind them all. And there are more wrongs in this world, and in every human life, than most people would like to admit.

At this point people are likely to say, "Ah, yes, but that's not true of everyone". Their argument is that not everyone has severed the connection with God. Hence, not everyone behaves badly.

In response, it is necessary to point out that wrong-doing is much wider and deeper in our world than we might, at first, want to admit.

If you ask a person who raises this objection, "Has anyone ever hurt you by something they've said or done?", they have only two options: to say yes, or to lie. If you follow this up by asking, "Have you ever hurt anybody else by something you've said or done?", they have the same two options: they can say yes, or they can lie. We've all done it. Sometimes the ones we hurt are the ones closest to us. No-one gets through life without broken relationships.

At this point, if you're having difficulty convincing someone of the universal reality of sin, one possible move is to be honest with them about yourself. I'm not suggesting that you should turn the conversation into an inappropriate confessional. But you can be honest enough to admit that you don't always live up to your own standards. You don't always succeed in doing what you should do. You can make this point without revealing all the gory details. "That failure is true of me", you might say. "What about you?"

If we go back to those two guidelines which Jesus says sum up all that God requires of us, and look carefully at the second one, we notice something significant. "You shall love your neighbour as yourself", says Jesus (Mark 12:31). Now that's a big call. Have you looked at your neighbour lately? Not easy to love. And loving your neighbour with the same kind of support and care and concern that you save for yourself ... well, that's a very hard ask indeed. The result is that we all break this vital rule (number two on God's summary of his Top Ten) not just by doing the wrong thing, but by failing to do the right thing.

Wrongdoing is universal. We've all done it, we all do it—either by hurting others, or by falling down in our obligations and failing to help others. It's doubtful that any of us gets through as much as a single day without some wrongdoing or relational failure. And we do wrong because our hearts are wrong.

Step 4

God's standard is not 'near enough is good enough'. God's standard requires not that we stop getting all the little things wrong, but that we give up our rebellion. What is needed is not a pass mark—a score above 50%—but repentance and forgiveness.

The assumption many people unconsciously make is

that God has a sort of pass mark, just like a school grade. No-one is going to score 100% in the test, but if you do well enough you'll be marked as a 'pass', not a 'fail'. The ones who fail are the criminal classes, the people who commit the truly horrible offences and appear on the nightly news. They are the ones condemned by God because they've fallen below the pass mark. They will end up in hell. The rest of us—and that's most of us—have scored a pass mark, and we'll get to heaven.

This is a lovely picture. Unfortunately it's total fiction. It's certainly not in the Bible. There's no evidence that God has lowered his standard. God is perfect, and God's standard is perfection.

But surely, people protest, God in loving kindness will give a pass to everyone who does their best?

Remember those Bible passages with which we began? The Bible doesn't sound as though God gives a 'passing grade' to the human race when it says, "no-one understands; no-one seeks for God. All have turned aside" (Rom 3:10-12). And Jesus doesn't sound as though he gives a 'passing grade' to the human heart and what it produces in human lives, when he says, "For from within, out of the heart of man, come evil thoughts, sexual immorality, theft, murder, adultery, coveting, wickedness, deceit, sensuality, envy, slander, pride, foolishness" (Mark 7:21-22). In other words, good, moral people who won't listen to God and won't obey God still fall short of God's standard—no matter how good and moral they are.

Imagine someone in the Old West of America who was an outlaw. This guy might be very good at being an outlaw. He's a crack shot, a good horseman, loyal to his gang leader and the other gang members. But he's still an outlaw. He's still a rebel against the lawful authority of the government. He might even be a kind and generous man as he stops to patch up a wounded fellow outlaw, but he's still an outlaw. He's someone who rejects the government's authority over the Old West.

From heaven's point of view, we are all outlaws. We are rebels and outlaws against heaven with a price on our heads. It doesn't matter whether we're 'good' outlaws or 'bad' outlaws—we're still outlaws.

Step 5

God has a right to demand these things of us because he made and owns us. God has a right to control every life and every part of every life. His standard is the one that counts, not ours.

The point needs to be made that we owe allegiance to God. God has the right to control every life, and every part of every life. Our maker and ruler is our owner.

God made us and the world around us. God placed us in this world for a purpose. We can't serve that purpose if we just get on with living our lives our own way. That is rebellion against God. That is what's wrong with the world. And that will finally catch up with us (that's the next point in our gospel outline).

Even though God hasn't made us as robots or puppets, we are still made by him, still loved by him, still supported and cared for by him every day—we still owe him everything we are and have. It is God who holds the molecules of matter together and causes the so-called 'laws of nature' to keep on working—and in that way God feeds and supports each one of us each day.

Our obligation to God is complete. Our offence against God is also complete.

Of course, there are many who simply will not be persuaded by these arguments. The reality is that no-one wants to admit human nature is corrupt and sinful and has a bent towards wrongdoing. Everyone finds that a very painful message to cope with. But the arguments and evidence are there—and are worth explaining, gently and respectfully, in order to lower one more barrier to the gospel being understood.

IN SUMMARY:

- The biblical definition of sin needs to be explained to replace the world's false definition of sin. Sin is not some people breaking some of the rules some of the time; it's all people rebelling against God by ignoring him, and running their lives their own way. That commonplace of life (running your own life) is sin; it's what killed Christ; it's what needs forgiveness.
- All the wrongs in the world go back to that big basic universe-sized wrong: human beings ignoring God and running their own lives. All the other wrongs and hurts flow from this in a basic cause-and-effect relationship.

- All those small wrongs are evidence of the big wrong (the big rebellion against God) that lies behind them all. There are more wrongs in this world, and in every human life, than most people would like to admit. Honesty demands that we should.
- God's standard is not 'near enough is good enough'. God's standard requires not that we stop getting all the little things wrong, but that we give up our rebellion. What is needed is not a 'pass mark' but repentance and forgiveness.
- God has a right to demand these things of us because he made and owns us. God has a right to control every life and every part of every life. His standard is the one that counts, not ours.

If you want to see how this world looks to God, picture the average teenager's room. The mess you see is caused by adolescent rebellion, rejecting the rules, and a degree of self-indulgent laziness.

We have all done to God's world what the average teenager has done to his room: made a mess of it. And for much the same reasons: rebellion, rejecting God's rule, and a good deal of self-indulgence.

DEFENDING SIN

Chapter 4

DEFENDING
JUDGEMENT

What the gospel says

God won't let us rebel forever. God cares enough about
humanity to take our rebellion seriously. He calls us to
account for our actions, because it matters to him that
we treat him, and other people, so poorly. In other
words, he won't let the rebellion go on indefinitely. So
the third point in our gospel outline tells us that God's
punishment for rebellion is death and judgement.

This judgement God passes against us is entirely just,
because he gives us exactly what we ask for. In rebelling
against God, we are saying to him, "Go away. I don't want
you telling me what to do. Just leave me alone."

This is precisely what God does. His judgement on
rebels is to withdraw from them, to cut them off from
himself—permanently. But since God is the source of
life and all good things, being cut off from him leads to

death and hell. God's judgement against rebels is an everlasting, God-less death.

It is a terrible thing to fall under the sentence of God's judgement. It is a prospect we all face, since we are all guilty of rebelling against God.

The Bible puts it plainly and clearly. God judges,

> ... inflicting vengeance on those who do not know God and on those who do not obey the gospel of our Lord Jesus. They will suffer the punishment of eternal destruction, away from the presence of the Lord and from the glory of his might ... (2 Thess 1:8-9)

Or, to make the same point more bluntly and succinctly:

> Man is destined to die once, and after that to face judgement. (Heb 9:27, NIV)

So, WHAT SORT OF OBJECTIONS are people likely to raise against this notion of judgement? I think the first objection is likely to be along the lines that God is just not like that.

No-one will openly admit it, but many people like to think of God as being like Santa Claus. In the end, everyone will be happy and get gifts. The argument is often that God is loving, and a loving God would not judge people. The mistake here is the assumption that 'loving' means 'easygoing'.

The picture people seem to have in their heads is that they'll stand before God and say, perhaps a little plaintively, "Look, I know I'm not perfect ... but I sort of did my best ...". They imagine that God will give a dismissive wave of his hand and say, "Ah, well, whatever. Come on in."

But if God did that he would be careless, not loving. To be loving means to care passionately.

God is not a dotty, forgetful grandparent who is a soft touch. God is God. God loves perfectly. Judgement is an expression of that love.

Parents who love their children discipline their children. That discipline is an expression of love. Because they love their kids, they want their kids to grow up with a good character, good habits and self-discipline. And so they provide guidelines and training, give the kids rules to be followed, and administer punishments for the breach of those rules. That's what loving parents do.

Parents who truly love their children look at their behaviour and either approve or disapprove. They pass judgement. Loving parents never say, "Ah, well, whatever ... I don't care what you do or how you behave." That's the opposite of love: indifference. Parents who don't love their kids just let them run wild. As long as the kids are not making a lot of noise, or irritating them in some way, the kids can do what they like.

The fact that God promises to judge us shows how much God loves us. God doesn't have the easygoing attitude of careless parents. God wants us to be all that we could and should be. That requires character development and good habits and guidelines and rules. It requires judgement as to how we have performed against God's requirements.

God looks at our behaviour and either approves or disapproves. He passes judgement **because** he loves us. Judgement is an expression of how much God cares for us and about us. That's really the answer to people who say that God is too loving to pass judgement. God passes judgement because he **is** loving.

The next objection might be that while people can believe lots of things, they can't believe that a loving God would send people to hell. And it does sound pretty horrible, doesn't it? But part of the reason it sounds so awful is that people have vague images in their minds of hell being a place of physical torments. So, how do we respond?

Well, the honest answer to this second objection is that the punishment fits the crime. In fact, even more than that—the punishment **is** the crime. We get what we want.

Human rebellion against God consists of refusing to submit to God's rule. In effect, by the way we live, we say to God, "No-one tells me what to do—not even God". The message we send, by the way we live our daily lives, is: "Don't bother me. Just leave me alone."

How should God respond to that message? Well, if we persist in sending that message to God throughout our lives—all the way from the cradle to the grave—what God does is to take us at our word. He treats us like adults, and takes our request, or demand, seriously.

God's judgement consists of giving us our choice, of allowing us to choose to live forever without him. And giving us our choice means (inevitably) banishing us from his immediate presence—since that's the demand we've expressed by the way we've lived.

'Hell' means being judged and moved "away from the presence of the Lord and from the glory of his might" (2 Thess 1:9). It is exile, or banishment. But that's what human beings keep asking for. What Jesus says at that decisive judgement to those who reject his rule is: "I never knew you; depart from me ..." (Matt 7:23). There's that note of exile (banishment) again.

Some people might respond by saying, "Well, that's okay ... I could cope with that". But it's not okay. It's hell.

We live in a world from which God is not absent. We cannot begin to imagine what the complete withdrawal of his presence would be like. Hell is not, as Sartre said, other people; hell is loneliness. And that's what people are choosing when they choose to be cut off from God, and from God's people, and from the light and love and life and purpose of the universe. The nearest picture of hell I can think of in this world is the solitary confinement cell. That's hell.

"Leave me alone!" we shout at God by the way we live our lives. Hell is being left alone. As I said: the punishment doesn't just fit the crime; the punishment **is** the crime. The offence is cutting yourself off from God. The punishment is being cut off from God.

Seen this way, we can say that hell is something we choose for ourselves.

There's a third important argument to make in defence of God's judgement: it's worth making the point that there must be justice in the universe.

We all, at some level, know this to be true. Unfairness, injustice, really bothers us at some deep level. When we become aware of a case of injustice we find ourselves saying, "It shouldn't be like this". There is a hunger in the human heart for the universe to be a just place. When horrible crimes are uncovered, we want someone to be brought to justice for the horror and the suffering. When a rapist or a murderer is given a short prison sentence, we are outraged. We want justice.

So, what are we to say about those cases where vicious and evil people seem to get away with their crimes? Do those who commit foul crimes against humanity, and who then die without facing a court, escape justice? Joseph Stalin died in his bed, of old age, having slaughtered some 15 million of the people he ruled as an absolute dictator. Pol Pot was never brought to justice for the killing fields of Cambodia. Hitler died by his own hand before he could face the war crimes tribunal at Nuremberg.

Did these men, and other lesser criminals who were never caught or punished, escape from justice? God's universal judgement assures us they did not. No-one escapes judgement.

Picture an evil man who is the head of an organized crime syndicate. Throughout his life he has ordered murders. He has had his rivals tortured and killed. Through his drug trafficking he has ruined countless lives, consigned people into a living hell, driven women into prostitution, and caused untold suffering. And then he dies at an old age, in his bed, surrounded by his weeping family—because the FBI never got enough evidence to bring him to trial.

Has he escaped? God promises that he has not. The books will be balanced. God promises us that the universe, in the end, is a just place. His universal judgement guarantees that. But of course, once judgement is universal, then **we**, as well as the Mafia Don, have to face it.

There is one final argument in support of this that's worth mentioning: Jesus teaches judgement. There is a widespread error that God's judgement is a topic of the Old Testament (or of Paul's letters), while Jesus is loving and forgiving. Nothing could be further from the truth. The one person in the Bible who teaches most about judgement and punishment is Jesus.

For instance, in Matthew 25 Jesus paints a vivid picture of what will happen when he returns to judge the world:

> "When the Son of Man comes in his glory, and all the angels with him, then he will sit on his glorious throne. Before him will be gathered all the nations, and he will separate people one from another as a shepherd separates the sheep from the goats. And he will place the sheep on his right, but the goats on the left ...
>
> Then he will say to those on his left, 'Depart from me, you cursed, into the eternal fire prepared for the devil and his angels'." (Matt 25:31-33, 41)

That's the voice of Jesus speaking. "Eternal fire" is the sort of poetic language the Bible uses to try to convey the horror of that final separation from God. Elsewhere Jesus calls it "destruction" (Matt 7:13) and "perishing" (John 3:16). The Jesus who teaches this then actually shows us the sheer horror of that hellish banishment when he cries out on the cross, "My God, my God, why have you forsaken me?" (Matt 27:46). Jesus is at that moment suffering the judgement and punishment that should fall on us. He is at that moment our substitute, facing our judgement and suffering our punishment. He is going through hell on our behalf. And as we look with horror on his agony, we see what it is we are calling upon ourselves by turning away from God, and asking God to withdraw from us completely.

So then, Jesus teaches about judgement, and shows us the horror of falling under God's judgement. Hence, there's no escape from the message of judgement by trying to say, "Jesus would not let that happen".

In summary:

- God's judgement is an expression of his love. God judges us because he loves us. If he didn't judge us it would mean that he didn't care about us.
- God's judgement is fair because the punishment that results is the punishment human beings, by their rebellion, have requested. Hell is something we choose for ourselves.
- If God did not pass universal judgement, the universe would be an unfair place. Countless cruel and horrible crimes would never be punished. By promising universal judgement, God is promising us that every crime, every wrongdoing, every fault,

failing and failure will be judged. The universe is ultimately just.

- Jesus teaches more about hell and judgement than any other person in the Bible.

The good news is that this is not the end. We've only reached the halfway point in 'the logic of the universe'.

DEFENDING JUDGEMENT

Chapter 5

DEFENDING JESUS

What the gospel says

Because of his great love and generosity, God did not leave us to suffer the consequences of our foolish rebellion. He did something to save us. He sent his own divine Son into our world to become a man—Jesus of Nazareth.

Unlike us, Jesus didn't rebel against God. He always lived under God's rule. He always did what God said, and so did not deserve death or punishment. Yet Jesus did die. Although he had the power of God to heal the sick, walk on water and even raise the dead, Jesus allowed himself to be executed on a cross.

Why?

Because by dying in our place he took our punishment and paid for our forgiveness.

The Bible rings with the incredible news that Jesus died as a substitute for rebels like us. The debt that we owed God, Jesus paid by dying in our place. He took the full force of God's justice on himself, so that forgiveness and pardon might be available to us.

All this is quite undeserved by us. It is a generous gift—a completely free gift—from start to finish. Here's how the Bible puts it:

> Christ died for sins once for all, the righteous for the unrighteous, to bring you to God. (1 Pet 3:18, NIV)

> He himself bore our sins in his body on the tree, that we might die to sin and live to righteousness. By his wounds you have been healed. (1 Pet 2:24)

THE BIGGEST PROBLEM we are likely to run into at this point is that people twist the truth about Jesus. Or else they unwittingly pass on distortions told by others—not knowing them to be lies.

There seems to be a whole industry that consists of twisting the truth about Jesus. In fact, there are some who seem to take pleasure in weaving a complex web of confusion around Jesus. It is important to be clear about what such people are denying. Often what they appear to be denying is a smokescreen and the key issue is not immediately apparent.

The 'Twisting the Truth About Jesus' industry often wants to deny that Jesus died on the cross, or that he performed any miracles, or that he came back from the dead. Smokescreen. Not the real issue. What they are really denying is that Jesus was and is God. That's the central issue. Once people accept that Jesus is God come into this world as a man, all the other issues cease to be a problem.

Now it's important to bear in mind that, according to surveys, there are many unchurched people who have no difficulty accepting the divinity of Jesus. With such people this issue doesn't need to be defended. All you need to do is point out that once you believe Jesus is God, there is logically no problem with Jesus performing miracles or coming back from the dead. Indeed, such things pretty much go with the territory of being God.

But where this is not accepted, what needs to be defended is the truth that Jesus claimed to be God and that his claim is true. Denying this is the Big Twist at the heart of the 'Twisting the Truth About Jesus' industry.

Sometimes this twist is very obvious (as in *The Da Vinci Code*), sometimes less so (as in the case of people who promote the so-called Gnostic 'gospels'[1] as if they had the same authority as Matthew, Mark, Luke and John). This 'Twisting the Truth About Jesus' industry gets a lot of space in the popular media. So it's against this that we need to defend the truth that Jesus really did claim to be God, and that his claim is true.

The place to start is by asking: does the Bible really

---

[1]   The Gnostic 'gospels' are a collection of writings dating from the early period of Christianity, but teaching salvation by the acquiring of secret knowledge, rather than through the death of Jesus.

record Jesus making this astonishing claim?

A lot of people would like to think that Jesus never made such an outrageous claim. They would like to think that Jesus was just a good man, a great teacher, a religious leader, a social reformer, a faith healer, or even a martyr. But the Bible does not leave us the option of saying he was 'just' these things.

His first followers recognized what Jesus was claiming, and acknowledged him as God. When those early followers worshipped him as God, Jesus accepted their worship as proper and appropriate (Matt 14:33). Indeed, he said that they ought to honour him as they honoured his Father, God (John 5:23). These followers were devout Jews who believed in the one and only creator God—yet they recognized Jesus as that one true God.

It is important to realize that in doing this, they were merely responding to the claim Jesus made for himself. Sometimes he made that claim directly, and sometimes indirectly.

The earliest of the four Gospels is most likely the Gospel of Mark, according to the best current scholarship. It records one occasion when a paralysed man was brought to Jesus to be healed:

> And they came, bringing to him a paralytic carried by
> four men. And when they could not get near him
> because of the crowd, they removed the roof above him,
> and when they had made an opening, they let down the
> bed on which the paralytic lay. And when Jesus saw
> their faith, he said to the paralytic, "My son, your sins
> are forgiven." Now some of the scribes were sitting

there, questioning in their hearts, "Why does this man speak like that? He is blaspheming! Who can forgive sins but God alone?" And immediately Jesus, perceiving in his spirit that they thus questioned within themselves, said to them, "Why do you question these things in your hearts? Which is easier, to say to the paralytic, 'Your sins are forgiven', or to say, 'Rise, take up your bed and walk'? But that you may know that the Son of Man has authority on earth to forgive sins"—he said to the paralytic—"I say to you, rise, pick up your bed, and go home." And he rose and immediately picked up his bed and went out before them all, so that they were all amazed and glorified God, saying, "We never saw anything like this!" (Mark 2:3-12)

The question Jesus asked the religious leaders was an impossible challenge for them. They knew, because the Old Testament teaches, that God alone is able to forgive sins. Jesus wanted them to understand that he exercised the power of God, because he **is** God. So he first forgave the man, and then healed his paralysis (in order to demonstrate his divine authority to forgive).

So the Bible records Jesus as claiming to be God in probably the very earliest of the Gospels to be written down, the Gospel of Mark.

There are only four possible reactions to such a claim. First, you could deny the Gospel records—saying they are later legends and not eyewitness history. Second, you could attack the character of Jesus by calling him a liar. Third, you might denigrate Jesus by calling him a lunatic. Fourth, you could acknowledge that he really made this claim and that he really backed it up—that he was and is the Lord God of creation who came in the form and flesh of a man.

More than half a century ago C. S. Lewis proposed that when we look at Jesus we are faced with three alternatives: is he a liar, or a lunatic, or the Lord?[2] Today I think we must add a fourth alternative: is Jesus a mere legend—invented, or falsified, by his early followers? This question is, perhaps, the dominant one today. In what follows I will look at those four options and consider them in turn. Jesus Christ: legend, liar, lunatic or Lord?

Is the Jesus of the Gospels a legend?

Those who promote this idea are really saying that Jesus was just a man, that he never claimed to be God, and that such claims were cooked up by later generations who, perhaps, wanted to use this claim about the divinity of Jesus for their own purposes.

At this point, I will not specifically address *The Da Vinci Code* since there are so many excellent books that already do so, such as *Is it Worth Believing?* by Greg Clarke.[3] However, the so-called Gnostic 'gospels'[4] do

---

[2]   You can find the argument in Book II, Chapter 3 of C. S. Lewis's *Mere Christianity*, Fontana Books, London and Glasgow, 1962 (1952).

[3]   Greg Clarke, *Is it Worth Believing?*, Matthias Media, Sydney, 2005.

[4]   See footnote 1, earlier in this chapter.

deserve a brief mention. Perhaps the best way to explain why they don't matter is with an historical parallel.

European settlement of Australia began in 1788 with the arrival of a convict fleet under Arthur Phillip to establish a penal colony. There are many published eyewitness reports of those early years—by Watkin Tench, David Collins, Arthur Phillip himself and others. If I sat down today, more than 200 years later, and forged an account of that early settlement that contradicted the historical eyewitness records we have, and if I signed my forgery in the name of one of the early settlers, what historical value would my forged document have?

If you said "None", you are correct.

That's what the so-called Gnostic 'gospels' are— forgeries written between 100 and 300 years after the time of Jesus. They have exactly zero value as historical records of Jesus. Why did the Gnostic philosophers who wrote these forgeries not sign their own names to them? Why did they dishonestly sign them in the names of first-century members of the Jesus circle? Because they were dishonest documents from day one.

There is really nothing more to be said about those so-called Gnostic 'gospels' except those two words—late forgeries.

That's the negative side of the story—what about the positive side? Is there positive evidence that in the Bible's account of Jesus we have reliable history and not later legends? The answer is: "Yes". We have the story about Jesus from eyewitnesses, and from those who consulted eyewitnesses. The sources are sound. The reports are early and accurate.

The earliest records we have of Jesus are not found in the Gospels but in the letters (the epistles) in the New Testament, written by such early followers of Jesus as Peter, Paul, John, James and Jude. Probably by around AD 49, at least three of those New Testament letters had already been written: Galatians, James and 1 Thessalonians. So these were written around 16 years after Jesus died. In historical terms, 16 years is a minute period of time. My memory of things that happened 16 years ago is quite clear. And if I forget, I have lots of friends who were, like me, adults 16 years ago, and who can also remember clearly.

By around AD 51, it's likely that 2 Thessalonians had also been written—just 18 years after the death of Jesus. Within the next ten years, most of the letters in the New Testament were written.

These very early letters tell us that:

1. Jesus was a Jew, and a descendant of both Abraham (Gal 3:16) and King David (Rom 1:3).
2. He was born and lived in relative poverty (2 Cor 8:9).
3. He had a brother named James (Gal 1:19).
4. He was gentle and meek (2 Cor 10:1).
5. His public work was mainly among Jews (Rom 15:8).
6. He was unfairly treated (Rom 15:3).
7. He was put on trial before the local Roman governor, Pontius Pilate (1 Tim 6:13).

8. He was executed (1 Thess 2:14-15).
9. He came back from the dead, and was seen alive by many of his early followers, sometimes alone and sometimes in groups (1 Cor 15:4-6).

That's not bad for an early list of facts about Jesus—written and distributed widely only a relatively short time after his life and death; a time when any errors or misrepresentations could be corrected by the host of eyewitnesses who were still alive, both friends and enemies. What Jesus said and did, and what happened to him, was public knowledge in Judea in those days. As one of his early followers said, these things were not "done in a corner" (Acts 26:26).

Those early letters all speak about Jesus as "the Lord"—meaning both the Christ (the Messiah, Israel's divinely designated king) and the Lord God of creation.

Then there are those four short biographies of Jesus: the Gospels of Matthew, Mark, Luke and John. They were written after the letters, and were either written by eyewitnesses or based on the reports of eyewitnesses. For instance, Luke, who according to tradition was Greek by birth and a doctor by training, begins his biography of Jesus with these words:

> Inasmuch as many have undertaken to compile a narrative of the things that have been accomplished among us, just as those who from the beginning were eyewitnesses and ministers of the word have delivered them to us, it seemed good to me also, having

followed all things closely for some time past, to write an orderly account for you, most excellent Theophilus, that you may have certainty concerning the things you have been taught. (Luke 1:1-4)

And everything in those four Gospels, or biographies, matches perfectly with what had already been written in those very early letters. It all fits together—the letters and Gospels in the New Testament confirm each other.

Then there are documents written by first-century historians who were enemies of both Jesus and his followers. Two Roman writers, Pliny and Tacitus, describe what the first Christians were like—followers of someone known as Jesus, who had been crucified under the Roman governor Pontius Pilate and who was said to have risen from the dead.

Most significantly, Pliny was disturbed because these Christians "prayed to Christ **as to a God**" (emphasis mine) and because the pagan temples were being deserted as more and more people became Christians.

A first-century Jewish historian named Josephus also described Jesus' life and teaching in some detail, including his death and reports of his resurrection.

Jesus, then, cannot be dismissed as a myth or invention. What we have in the New Testament comes from the 'Jesus generation': those who actually knew Jesus face-to-face, who saw and heard him.

The confirmation comes in the form of the perfect match that exists between the early Christian letters, the four Gospels, and early secular historians. This triple confirmation shows that what we are dealing with cannot possibly be later legends. These are the facts about Jesus that were believed by the people who knew him.

So we are stuck with a reliable record in which Jesus claimed to be God.

Is the Jesus of the Gospels a liar?

This raises the second question: when Jesus made this claim, was he lying? Perhaps, someone might suggest, he thought his teaching would have more authority (and would more likely be remembered) if he made this outrageous claim.

The impossibility of this is best summed up by C. S. Lewis—the former professor of literature at Cambridge University I cited earlier—who wrote:

> I am trying here to prevent anyone saying that really foolish thing that people often say about Him: "I'm ready to accept Jesus as a great moral teacher, but I don't accept His claim to be God". That is the one thing we must not say. A man who was merely a man and said the sort of things Jesus said would not be a great moral teacher. He would either be a lunatic—on a level with a man who says he is a poached egg—or else he would be the Devil of Hell. You must make your choice. Either this man was, and is, the Son of God: or else a madman or something worse.[5]

---

5   C. S. Lewis, op. cit., pp. 52-53.

When we read the Gospels, what strikes us is the authority of Jesus. We notice his moral purity and dignity. We read his parables and notice his astonishing insight into the human heart. We notice the powerful effect he has on those around him. His enemies are powerless to arrest him until he allows himself to be taken. Even his closest followers stand in awe of him.

Whatever such a man needed to do, he did not need to lie.

The moral stature of Jesus is beyond question. Even those who reject his own claim to be God continue to respect Jesus as a great moral teacher. During his lifetime his moral integrity was never questioned. It is impossible for such a morally conscientious man to tell such a lie—since the claim to be God, if untrue, is not just a lie, but a lie of monstrous proportions.

Jesus, then, was not a mere legend, and not a manipulative liar.

Is the Jesus of the Gospels a lunatic?

Is it possible that Jesus was self-deluded, that his mind was disturbed—that he was some sort of megalomaniac with a God-complex?

Again, the evidence shows otherwise. If someone claims to be, and seriously believes himself to be, Napoleon, then the rest of his behaviour tends to be of a piece with this delusion. His delusion affects the whole of his personality. There are no great surgeons or scientists who think they are Napoleon. They know who they are, and are not confused about their own identities. Severe delusion about one's personal identity means one cannot function professionally or socially. But Jesus functioned brilliantly as a professional teacher. Socially he was comfortable, poised, composed and dignified. None of the eyewitness reports matches a lunatic who mistakes himself for God.

Remember, too, the impact he had on those around him. If he was a mentally unbalanced fanatic, the Jewish authorities could have safely ignored him. If his teaching had not been delivered with the power of clear, cool sanity, the Roman authorities would never have felt the need to execute him. Mad? No, the sanest man who ever lived.

Is the Jesus of the Gospels the Lord of creation?

So, Jesus was no legend, no liar, and no lunatic. All that remains is that he was exactly who he claimed to be: the Lord of creation, the creator God, the true and living God come in human form to rescue and to rule. That means people have to take his claims seriously— including his claim about why he came, and what his death accomplishes:

> "For even the Son of Man came not to be served but to serve, and to give his life as a ransom for many." (Mark 10:45)

"I am the good shepherd. The good shepherd lays down his life for the sheep." (John 10:11)

It seems to me that most of the issues raised in the popular media about the death and resurrection of Jesus, or his miracles, can be settled by addressing this larger question of whether Jesus is who he claimed to be: God—in the form and flesh of a man, but still with the power and authority of God.

That he **is** God is established by the early eyewitness historical records that show Jesus making this claim and backing it up by his actions, and by the sheer impossibility of the liar or lunatic charges.

But why did he have to die?

However, there is one more question some people might want to ask. Why did Jesus have to die so that God could forgive us? Why couldn't God just take a pen, so to speak, and scratch out the records of wrongdoing against our names? Why was this awful death necessary?

This question is really asking: couldn't God give up on being just? Couldn't God turn the universe into an unjust place in order to forgive us? The answer is that there is one thing God cannot do—namely, be untrue to his own character. God is perfectly just as well as perfectly loving. In a sense, God had a problem. How could he lovingly forgive without ceasing to be perfectly just? His answer was the cross.

It has often been pictured in the following way. A magistrate was sitting on the bench in the district court when his own daughter was brought before him charged with a traffic offence. The charge was proved by the police prosecutor. The magistrate had sworn to uphold the law, so he had no choice but to impose the penalty the law required. This was a large fine, with a three-month prison sentence if the fine wasn't paid. He imposed the sentence. But knowing that his daughter, a student, couldn't possibly afford the fine, he then stepped down from the bench and paid it himself.

As a magistrate he imposed the fine; as a father he paid the fine. Justice was upheld, the penalty was paid, but his daughter didn't have to go to prison.

On a small scale, that's a picture of what God has done on the cross. There, God the Son dies to pay for the damage done by human beings, so that those human beings can be forgiven.

To see the compelling logic of this, it's necessary to understand that forgiveness is not just a nothing. Forgiveness is not casual and insignificant. Forgiveness is always costly, and the one who does the forgiving is the one who pays the cost. If you forgive a friend or relative for something, it will cost you. Sometimes the cost is small: just a feeling of hurt pride, or public embarrassment, or inconvenience. But if what needs forgiving involves real damage, then the cost can be considerable.

In my little book *Journey Towards God* [6] I tell the

---

6   Kel Richards, *Journey Towards God*, Beacon Communications, Sydney, 1999, pp. 90-92.

following story to explain the cost of forgiveness. Dave was driving from Sydney to Melbourne. After being on the road for several hours he stopped at a small town for a break and a cup of coffee. As he pulled out from the kerb to continue his journey a large, four-wheel drive vehicle came roaring around the corner and slammed into the front of Dave's car.

He got out and inspected the damage. It was superficial, but would be expensive to fix. He walked over to the four-wheel drive. In the driver's seat was a teenager. Dave just wanted to exchange insurance details and get back on the road, so he asked the young man for his driver's licence. The reply was, "I don't have a licence. I'm only fifteen. This car belongs to a friend. I only got in and drove it to impress a girl."

Dave had to work out what to do. At first he suggested driving to the police station and letting them sort it out. The young man pleaded with Dave not to get him into trouble with the law. Then Dave proposed driving to the boy's home and talking to his father. If the father would pay for the damage, that would be the end of the matter. The boy pleaded with Dave not to do this. His father was a violent man, and the boy would be beaten if his father found out.

"Well," said Dave, "what do you suggest we do about it?"

"Can't you just let me go?" pleaded the boy. "I've had an awful fright. I'll never do it again, I promise. Please ... can't you forgive me ... let me go ... just this once?"

Dave let him go. He told the boy to take the four-wheel drive straight back to his friend's place and

DEFENDING JESUS

promise not to get behind the wheel again until he had a licence. The young man drove away, greatly relieved.

But that wasn't the end of it. It couldn't be the end of it, because there was still damage to Dave's car that had to be repaired. Someone had to pay for that damage. Dave knew when he let the kid go that he would have to pay for it himself.

What Jesus has done is to pay for our damage. Even if we ask God to forgive us, and God says "Yes", there is still all that damage that has to be paid for. By rejecting God's rule, and becoming the 'god' of our own lives, we have done damage to ourselves, and to other people, and to relationships, and to God's creation around us. It's a lot of damage.

As he was dying on the cross there was a moment— towards the end—when Jesus cried out: "My God, my God, why have you forsaken me?" (Matt 27:46). Can you understand what was happening there? At that moment Jesus was going through that terrible, ultimate, final separation from God that is death and hell. He didn't deserve it, but we do, and he went through it on our behalf.

That death is what pays for our damage; it reconciles us to God; it deals with the judgement we would otherwise have to face.

Forgiveness is always costly. The person who does the forgiving is the one who pays the price. That is why Jesus had to die if we were to be forgiven.

On the cross, the perfect justice and the perfect love of God meet.

> For while we were still weak, at the right time Christ died for the ungodly. For one will scarcely die for a righteous person—though perhaps for a good person one would dare even to die—but God shows his love for us in that while we were still sinners, Christ died for us. (Rom 5:6-8)

That is the answer to the question, "Why did Jesus have to die?"

IN SUMMARY:

- Jesus' claim to be God is not a later legend but is found in the early eyewitness records that make up the New Testament.
- Jesus cannot be dismissed as a liar in the light of his moral teaching and authority.
- Jesus cannot be dismissed as a lunatic in the light of how seriously he was taken by both his followers and his enemies.
- Jesus, therefore, is who he claimed to be: God come in human form to die for his people, to pay for their sins.
- And Jesus had to die—to pay for the damage caused by our wrongdoing—if we were ever to be forgiven.
- On the cross, God's perfect justice and perfect love meet.

And, of course, the story does not end there ...

Chapter 6

DEFENDING THE RESURRECTION

What the gospel says

God raised Jesus again as the ruler of the world.

The fifth point in our gospel outline says that God has accepted Jesus' death as payment in full for our sins, and raised him from the dead. The risen Jesus is now what humanity was always meant to be: God's ruler of the world.

As God's ruler, Jesus has also been appointed God's judge of the world. The Bible promises that one day, he will return to call all of us to account for our actions.

In the meantime, Jesus offers us new life, both now and eternally. Our sins can be forgiven through Jesus' death, and we can make a fresh start with God, no longer as rebels but as friends. In this new life, God himself comes to live within us by his Spirit. We can experience the joy of a new relationship with God.

What's more, when we are pardoned through Jesus' death, we can be quite sure that when Jesus does return to judge, we will be acceptable to him. The risen Jesus will give us eternal life, not because we have earned it but because he has died in our place.

Here's how the Bible puts it:

> "... because he has fixed a day on which he will judge the world in righteousness by a man whom he has appointed; and of this he has given assurance to all by raising him from the dead." (Acts 17:31)

> In his great mercy he has given us new birth into a living hope through the resurrection of Jesus Christ from the dead. (1 Pet 1:3, NIV)

THE PROBLEM HERE IS THAT some people will have trouble with the resurrection, and will raise objections.

However, once again, bear in mind that there are surveys showing that large numbers of people have no problem with the idea that Jesus came back from the dead. So this is not an issue to be argued over and defended unnecessarily. The reasons for believing in this (and they are good, strong reasons) need only be brought out if you find yourself talking to someone who raises a genuine objection.

This is a case where it is the unbeliever who is likely to appeal to observation and common sense. There's not much traffic going on in graveyards. At least, the traffic is all in. None of it is out. Once those corpses are buried, they stay there. The dead stay dead. That's just observation and common sense. That's the common argument against the resurrection of Jesus Christ.

Observation and common sense are usually helpful guides, but they don't apply in this case because the resurrection of Jesus is a unique event. Nothing like it has ever happened before or since. You can't apply the normal laws of observation to something that happened only once. To observe it, you have to be there. And we weren't.

Those people Jesus raised from the dead (such as Lazarus, and the son of the widow of Nain, and Jairus' daughter) were resuscitated corpses. Each of them eventually died and was buried.

Jesus was no resuscitated corpse. Jesus was raised immortal—never to die again. The body he had immediately after his resurrection is the body he still has. It's the same body we will see when he returns. Paul calls it a *sōma pneumatikon*—a "spiritual body" (1 Cor 15:44). And Jesus is the one and only example of this happening (so far) in human history. That's why an appeal to observation and common sense can't settle this matter. Instead, we can appeal to the evidence that something remarkable (something utterly 'one off') did happen on this one special occasion. We will trace the Bible's argument mainly through the closing chapters of John's Gospel.

Jesus really died

One of the common lies told about Jesus these days is that he did not die on the cross. This claim is part of Islamic belief, and it's trotted out again in *The Da Vinci Code*. It is nonsense.

In the first place, Jesus was put to death by expert executioners. Roman death squads knew what they were doing. It was a disciplined army, and its execution squads were highly experienced experts. The claim that Jesus might have survived their expert attentions is ludicrous.

Then to make sure he was dead, the Roman soldiers thrust a spear into his side, and blood and water flowed out. Doctors say this shows that the spear pierced the stomach (the source of the watery fluid) and the upper chest (the source of most of the blood). If the crucifixion didn't kill Jesus, that spear thrust most certainly did (John 19:31-37).

After the soldiers pronounced Jesus to be dead, Joseph of Arimathea asked the Roman Governor Pilate for permission to bury the body. Pilate sent a message back to the execution squad to check that Jesus was really dead. In the Roman army a request from the Governor could not be ignored or treated lightly. So they checked. And then they sent a message back to Pilate saying, yes, he was really dead (Mark 15:44-45).

There is no room for doubt. Jesus really died on the cross.

Jesus' tomb was empty

The one really startling historical fact is that 36 hours after Jesus' execution, the tomb in which he was buried was found to be empty (John 20:1-18).

If there had been any doubt about this, the temple authorities who had conspired to have Jesus killed would have pointed to an undisturbed tomb. Or they could have produced the corpse of Jesus, and destroyed the young Christian movement in its infancy by hanging the rotting corpse of Jesus over the city gates of Jerusalem. They didn't because they couldn't. The tomb was empty. The corpse had vanished.

So widespread was the knowledge of the empty tomb at the time, that the temple authorities had to bribe the guards to spread a lie: "Tell people, 'His disciples came by night and stole him away while we were asleep'" (Matt 28:13). It was never a very convincing lie. You don't have to be the clever young television attorney to ask on cross-examination, "If you were asleep, how do you know what happened?"

Not only was the tomb empty but the grave clothes were lying there—laid out on the ground, only with no corpse inside them (John 20:6-7).

The disciples did not expect the resurrection

In response to suggestions that the resurrection was a plot or hoax pulled off by the disciples, it's worth pointing out that the disciples were caught entirely by surprise. When

Mary discovered the tomb to be empty her first thought was not, "Oh, silly me, that's right, he said he would rise again". Not at all. Instead she assumed the body had been stolen. When she ran to wake Peter and John and tell them that the body had vanished, they didn't say, "Calm down, it's just the promised resurrection", and then roll over and go back to sleep. Not at all. They ran in a wild panic to the now empty tomb (John 20:1-9).

Later, alone in the garden, Mary didn't see the gardener and think it was Jesus. She saw Jesus and mistook him for the gardener (John 20:11-18). Then, when Thomas was told by ten of his closest friends that they had all seen Jesus risen from the dead, he responded sceptically and said he would not believe until he touched the wounds (John 20:24-25).

The one thing we can be certain of is that, far from cooking up a conspiracy, the disciples were taken by surprise by Jesus' resurrection.

The risen Jesus was not a ghost or a phantom

When Mary encountered the risen Jesus in the garden, she clearly did not want to let him go again. So Jesus had to say, "Do not cling to me" (John 20:17), perhaps gently prising away her clutching arms as he spoke.

Then he offered his wounds to Thomas to reach out and touch, if he wished to do so (John 20:27). Later still, by Lake Galilee, Jesus cooked food for the disciples and ate with them (John 21:12-13).

Whatever form his body took, he was certainly no mere ghost or phantom or spirit.

The resurrection appearances of Jesus were not hallucinations

According to the textbooks, an hallucination is a chemical disturbance in a person's brain. For that reason, hallucinations cannot be shared. If the chemistry of your brain is causing you to see pink elephants, I won't see them—even if I'm in the same room, standing beside you. That's because it's all happening inside your head.

But Jesus appeared repeatedly to groups of people. He appeared to a group of women in the garden (Matt 28:9-10); to two disciples walking to Emmaus (Luke 24:13-35); to ten men in an upper room (John 20:19-23); eight days later to eleven of them (John 20:26-29); some time later to seven of them beside Lake Galilee (John 21:1-23); and, on one occasion, to as many as 500 of his disciples at one time (1 Cor 15:6).

Whatever these resurrection appearances were, they could not possibly have been hallucinations.

Not a lie or legend

To these arguments, spelled out in the Bible, we can add that the resurrection of Jesus was not a lie invented by his followers.

Most of those early followers of Jesus—the people who had claimed to see the risen Jesus and to have spoken with him—died painful martyr's deaths. They were killed for what they claimed.

No-one will die for a lie. For a truth—especially an important truth—a committed man or woman might lay down their life, but not for a story they know to be a lie.

The movement Jesus founded did not die

Finally, there is one more argument that I have found helpful on some occasions.

People who want to deny the resurrection of Jesus Christ have to (somehow) explain the spread of Christianity around the world. In most cities, there are churches all over the place. How did they come to be there? The name of Jesus Christ is known on every continent on earth, and Christianity is the largest faith in the world. How can this be explained?

This is a puzzle for unbelievers, because when Jesus was executed by Roman soldiers in AD 33 he had only a small number of followers (perhaps around 500). They were not rich or powerful or important people. For the most part they were tradesmen, small businessmen or minor public servants. Yet within half a lifetime, 30 years, Christians had become so numerous and so well-known that the Roman Emperor Nero, looking for a scapegoat, could blame the Christians for the great fire of Rome.

How did the small, depressed, disheartened, defeated group of men and women, who each talked about going back to their old trades, suddenly become this dynamic band that turned the Roman Empire on its ear? Something must have happened to them, something stunning and dramatic, something like ... well ... like their leader coming back from the dead.

At the time when Jesus was executed, there were other charismatic local leaders who claimed to be a messiah of some sort. Where are their churches and their followers today? Within Judaism there were various other movements at the time (the Sadducees, the Pharisees, the Essenes)—where are those movements today? How come they don't dominate the globe in the way that Christianity does?

And there were many powerful pagan religions at the time (the worship of Mithras, the worship of Diana, and others)—where are their temples? Why have they died out, and why has Christianity not only survived but spread to become the dominant faith on this planet?

There is something going on here that a merely human movement cannot explain—something like Jesus coming back from the dead, and empowering his followers with new life.

There is a useful contrast here with Muhammad, the founder of Islam. He died, peacefully in his bed, at the age of 62. By the time of his death, his followers had won a military conquest that gave them control of the whole Arabian peninsular, and Islam had tens of thousands of followers. It is hardly surprising that Islam survived Muhammad's death.

But it **is** surprising that Christianity—a small, powerless movement, in a remote corner of the Roman Empire—survived the death of Jesus. Only in the case of Christianity did the founder die young, leaving a small, frightened, disorganized group of followers. Yet they were somehow so galvanized that their faith swept the known world. The name of Jesus **should** have been largely forgotten by now, perhaps remembered only by a few scholars who study the remote corners of ancient history. Instead, followers of Jesus can now be found in every place on the planet.

The point is that the beginning of Christianity is unlike the beginning of any of the other major world religions. Christianity is not, for a start, the religion of a particular nation or ethnic group. Thus, it is not like Judaism, or Islam, or Hinduism in India, Buddhism in Japan or Confucianism in China. Christianity thrives in countless nations and among every ethnic group in the world.

The famous atheist David Hume once proposed that the only grounds for accepting a miracle would be that any alternative explanation would be even more unlikely (or more unpersuasive) than the miracle itself. Well, it seems to me that the miracle of the resurrection meets Hume's criterion: trying to explain the spread of Christianity **without** the resurrection of Jesus requires a bigger, and more inexplicable, miracle than the resurrection itself.

IN SUMMARY:

- Jesus really died on the cross. Roman execution squads didn't make that sort of mistake, and the evidence is that they certainly didn't in this case.
- The tomb was certainly empty. If it was not, the enemies of Jesus would have turned it to their

advantage. They didn't, because they couldn't—the tomb was empty.

- The disciples did not expect the resurrection. Far from engaging in some conspiracy or plot, they were caught completely by surprise.
- Jesus was no mere ghost or phantom or spirit. His followers could touch him, and he ate with them. His risen body was real and solid.
- Jesus appeared alive to groups of his followers repeatedly over more than a month following his resurrection—and these appearances can't be dismissed as hallucinations.
- The story of the resurrection is not a legend or a lie invented by the first followers of Jesus, because most of them died a painful martyr's death for telling exactly that story. Not one of the first followers of Jesus ever recanted and said, "We made it up"— because they didn't.
- The very existence and spread of Christianity around the globe is impossible to explain without the miracle of the resurrection to empower and inspire it.

And it is from these well-supported facts that the great challenge of the gospel comes ...

Chapter 7

DEFENDING THE CHALLENGE

What the gospel says

The last of the six points in our gospel outline spells out the challenge that arises from the first five, namely, that there are only two ways to live: our way or God's way. Those two options exhaust the possibilities.

Our way means that we continue rejecting God's rule, and continue trying to run life our own way without him. Sadly, this is the option that many people persist in. The result is that we remain condemned by God. Unless we turn around and change course, we continue to face death and judgement.

If we continue in our way (by the way we live, ignoring him), God gives us what we are asking for. He condemns us for our rejection of his rightful rule over our lives. We not only have to put up with the messy consequences of rejecting God here and now, but we face the dreadful prospect of an eternity of separation from him, without life or love or relationship.

The alternative is God's way. That means submitting to Jesus as our ruler.

For those of us who have realized that our situation is hopeless, there is a lifeline. If we turn back to God and appeal for mercy, trusting in Jesus' death and resurrection, then everything changes. The result is that we are forgiven by God and given eternal life as a free gift. God wipes our slate clean. He accepts Jesus' death as payment for our sins, and freely and completely forgives us. He pours his own Spirit into our hearts and grants us a new life that stretches past death and into forever. We are no longer rebels, but part of God's own family as his adopted sons and daughters.

From the moment we turn from our way to God's way, we live with Jesus as our ruler—our Captain, our Commander-in-Chief.

This is how the Bible puts it:

> Whoever believes in the Son has eternal life, but whoever rejects the Son will not see life, for God's wrath remains on him. (John 3:36, NIV)

> "For God so loved the world, that he gave his only Son, that whoever believes in him should not perish but have eternal life." (John 3:16)

As a result, the choice between the two ways to live could not possibly be clearer:

OUR WAY:	GOD'S NEW WAY:
• Reject the ruler—God	• Submit to Jesus as our ruler
• Try to run life our own way	• Rely on Jesus' death and resurrection

Result:	*Result:*
• Condemned by God	• Forgiven by God
• Facing death and judgement	• Given eternal life

At this point we need, gently and respectfully, to ask the unbeliever: which of these two ways represents the way you're living now? And which of these two ways represents the way you'd like to live?

BUT IF THEY STILL HAVE QUESTIONS and challenges at this point, what are they likely to be?

Well, there is really only one question that might arise at this point: "Is there no other option?" But this one issue can emerge in two different ways.

I don't know

It will sometimes come up in the form of the unbeliever not wanting just two boxes and having to tick either one or the other. What they want is a 'Don't know' box. They really want to believe that there are more options.

Sometimes the hesitations or questions at this point

revolve around the narrowness of the challenge. "Surely", they might say, "God is broader than that? Surely I don't have to make up my mind now? If I fell under a bus in half an hour I'm sure", they protest, "that God would know that I believed in him, that I was sincerely doing my best, and that I was genuinely wrestling with the 'our way/God's way' thing".

What such objectors are looking for is a way to dodge the challenge. The answer is that when it comes to how we stand with God, there is no neutral territory. There is no spiritual Switzerland; there is no fence to sit on.

The real answer is that "I don't know" is an answer.

Looking at the two options ('our way/God's way') and saying, "I don't know" or "I'll think about it later" is really a firm decision in favour of our way, and against God's way.

Picture it as sitting on the wrong train, going in the wrong direction: until a change is made, the traveller is still on the wrong track going the wrong way. Something positive has to be done to change that. Doing nothing is a positive decision to keep going in the wrong direction—travelling down the death track (the 'separation from God' track) and getting closer to death at the steady speed of one day every 24 hours. Deciding nothing is saying "No" to God.

What about other religions?

The second way this issue comes up can be in the form of a protest against the exclusivity of Jesus. "But surely you're not saying", the protestor cries, "that all the nice, sincere Buddhists, Hindus, Muslims and the rest are going to hell?"

The answer is that people are going where they want to go. Those who choose to be disconnected from God in this life, in this world, will be disconnected from God forever—that's spiritual death, or hell if you prefer.

"But hang on", the protestor continues. "It's very narrow-minded of you to say that Jesus is the only way to reconnect with God. Jesus can't be the exclusive way to God. There must be other ways to come home to God, not just the Jesus way."

The answer is that it's Jesus who makes this claim, not us. "I am the way, and the truth, and the life", said Jesus. "No-one comes to the Father except through me" (John 14:6). So those who reject the notion that there are only two ways to live must recognize that they are calling Jesus a liar. That's a fairly heavy thing to say to someone, but it's the truth.

It can be worth pointing out that this is God's call, not our call. It's not the case that God has said to us, "How would you like to come home to me? Pick your own way." That hasn't happened. God has said, "Like this". So it's either "like this", or we fail to get home to the security of God's friendship and God's forgiveness.

We must turn back to God in the way that God requires and has provided. And that means Jesus. It is God who is being exclusive at this point.

Sometimes the protestor will say at this point, "Well, that's just because you grew up in a Christian society.

Why couldn't it be the case that God speaks to Christians through Christ, to Buddhists through Buddha, to Muslims through Muhammad and so on?"

The answer is: "Only Jesus died". The only doorway to heaven is marked 'Forgiveness'. And Jesus is that door. Only Jesus can forgive us because only Jesus died in our place to pay for our wrongdoings. Buddha didn't die for Buddhists. Confucius didn't die for his followers. Muhammad didn't die for Muslims. L. Ron Hubbard didn't die for Scientologists.

Jesus alone took the weight of our rebellion and wrongdoings upon his shoulders and died for us. Only Jesus died our death, suffered our punishment, and purchased our forgiveness.

And only Jesus came back from the dead as the conqueror of death and the giver of new life.

These historical facts are exclusively true of Jesus, and make Jesus the exclusive way back to God. Jesus is the way God has provided (at unbelievable cost) for us to come home: "God shows his love for us in that while we were still sinners, Christ died for us" (Rom 5:8).

God's way is God's way. We're either in it or out of it. That's why there are only two ways.

One final objection is sometimes raised: "But what about people who haven't heard about Jesus? What will happen to them?"

The answer is that the Bible doesn't tell us, so we don't know. However, we do know God's character so we can trust God absolutely. Whatever is right is what will happen. God's character guarantees that.

But this is not usually a genuine objection: it's a smoke-screen. The real answer is: "You've now heard about Jesus, so, whatever happens with others, you can't use the 'ignorance excuse'. If you choose to continue living your way, and refuse to turn to God's way, you will have no excuses when you stand before God in judgement."

We have enough information to make the right decision. God will do whatever he will do for others but for us, it's our own eternal destiny that hangs in the balance.

IN SUMMARY:

- The only objection at this point is to the narrowness of the choice: just two ways.
- To those who want a third option ('Don't know'), the answer is that the 'I-won't-make-a-decision-now' option is a decision to remain cut off from God—a 'non-decision' is a decision against God.
- To those who want some way other than Jesus to get to heaven, the answer is that Jesus alone has died and risen again—no-one else has done that, so no-one else is qualified to forgive us and bring us home to God.
- To those who say, "What about those who haven't heard of Jesus?", the answer is that this is a smokescreen. Those who haven't heard are safe in the hands of a perfect God. But you have heard, you can't plead ignorance, and you have only two choices: your way or God's way.

Chapter 8

FOUR BIG ISSUES

IN THE PAST SIX CHAPTERS, we've looked at the main points involved in defending the gospel. However, there are some non-gospel issues that may come up and get in the way of the gospel being heard. This chapter will look at four of those, and what we might usefully say about them:

- Religion
- Church
- Suffering
- Truth

Religion

I am convinced that Christianity is not a 'religion'—in the sense in which that word is most commonly used today. The *Longman Dictionary of Contemporary English* (a dictionary designed for those learning English as a second language—and, hence, especially sensitive to contemporary usage) defines 'religion' as "a particular system of belief and all the ceremonies and duties that are related to it".

And it's possible to go further, and to say that in the minds of most people in Western culture (in nations such as Britain, Australia and the US) 'religion' particularly means those "ceremonies and duties".

Culturally the role that 'religion', in this sense, plays in Western societies resembles the role played by hobbies. Some people are religious, others collect stamps. Some people take up religion as the interest that occupies at least some of their free time. Others go fishing or abseiling.

In societies with high church attendance levels, such as parts of the United States, 'religion' ("ceremonies and duties") in the form of churchgoing is what occupies Sunday morning leisure time.

This contemporary meaning of 'religion' becomes clearer when we notice that this word 'religion' covers Buddhism, Islam, Hinduism, Judaism, Confucianism, Shintoism, Mormonism and any and all brands and types of Christianity. People who call themselves witches and warlocks (practitioners of 'Wicca') want their system of "ceremonies and duties" to be officially recognized as a 'religion'.

Perhaps 100 or 150 years ago it might have been possible to talk about 'true religion' (meaning the gospel). Such language is meaningless in contemporary Western society.

'Religion' has now come to mean pretty much what the word 'idolatry' means in the Bible—because the vast majority of "ceremonies and duties" (lumped together under the word 'religion') are "the work of human hands" (Deut 4:28). As such they are condemned by God in the strongest possible terms.

For this reason it seems to me important not to try to defend biblical Christianity against 'other religions'. Biblical Christianity is not a religion. It doesn't belong in the same box as Islam, Buddhism, Confucianism and all the rest. The basic principles for talking about 'religion' with unbelievers are these:

- Religions are things human beings invent (often to avoid God).
- God is not religious—and doesn't want us to be religious.
- God is interested in relationship, not religion.

While religions are about "ceremonies and duties", biblical Christianity is not. Biblical Christianity is about our relationship with God ("you shall love the Lord your God with all your heart and with all your soul and with all your mind and with all your strength"—Mark 12:30) and our relationships with each other ("You shall love your neighbour as yourself"—Mark 12:31). Certain actions may be involved, but they are not "duties" in the religious sense. They spring from the underlying relationship.

Back in 1967, Fritz Ridenour published a book called *How to Be a Christian Without Being Religious.*[1] My point

---

1   Fritz Ridenour, *How to Be a Christian Without Being Religious,* G/L Regal Books, Glendale, California, 1967.

exactly. If an unbeliever says, "I'm not interested in religion", the best response is: "Neither am I ... and what's more, God doesn't want you to be religious either".

Sometimes I've had an acquaintance or colleague say to me, "Now, Kel, you're religious, aren't you?"—to which my response is always, "No, I'm not religious ... I'm a Christian".

In the muddled, ill-informed Western culture in which we live, 'religion' in the minds of most people means various groups of people, each with their own different ceremonies and duties, who are after the same goal (knowing God or finding peace or whatever) but who hate each other for going about this in ways different from their own.

The images the word 'religion' is likely to evoke in the minds of unbelievers are: stained glass windows, organ music, choirs, dotty old clergymen, maiden aunts, dishonest televangelists, papal pomp and ceremony in television news reports, priests who sexually abuse children, a patriarchal plot to suppress women and hide the truth about Jesus, and so on.

None of this has anything to do with the loving maker and ruler of the universe who sent his own dearly beloved Son to die as a ransom for many—the good shepherd laying down his life for his sheep.

A friend of mine who has done a lot of evangelism among business executives tells me he often finds that people who are dismissive of 'religion' are still interested in Jesus and the Bible. The gospel of Jesus Christ, crucified and risen, is not a 'religion' and if we can avoid that particular confusion and muddle then we will be helping people to see more clearly who Jesus is and why he came.

Church

If anything, 'church' is an even more muddled word than 'religion' these days. Consider for a moment the many different ways in which the word 'church' is used today. 'Church' can mean:

1. A building: "The church is on the corner of Smith and Brown Streets."
2. A meeting: "Church starts at ten o'clock."
3. A membership: "Anne has joined Hurstville Presbyterian Church."
4. A denomination: The Catholic Church, the Baptist Church, etc.
5. A profession: "John has gone into the Church."
6. All the Christians in the world: often labelled "The invisible, indivisible, universal church", although this language is only ever used by Christians, not by unbelievers.
7. A secular variation of (6): all denominations plus all religious institutions. This is what unbelievers usually mean when they speak about "the Church"—as in, "The Church should do something about global warming".
8. The collection of things that I call 'my local church': this usually means the members, the meetings, the buildings, and the staff that—collectively—make up 'my local church'.
9. The Roman Catholic denomination: this is what Catholics mean by "the Church".

There may be more, but that's enough different meanings, and enough muddle, to be going on with.

Much that was said under the heading of 'religion' applies here too: we don't want confusion and muddle about 'church', especially vaguely negative feelings, to get in the way of an unbeliever seeing who Jesus is and why he came.

To many people in the Western world, 'church' involves a vaguely intimidating building, oddly dressed clergy, boring 'services' they remember sitting through (perhaps at weddings or funerals), and an activity the media constantly reports to be 'dying'.

This is not the place to spell out in detail the biblical doctrine of 'church' (and so sort out all these muddled meanings and odd impressions). But I should at least remind you that the Greek word usually translated 'church' is *ekklesia* which, literally, means 'gathering' or 'assembly'. All that we need to bear in mind for the moment is that in practice, 'church' is that group of people we meet with regularly to study the Bible, to pray with, and to mutually encourage and support. These are the people with whom we 'gather' or 'assemble'.

That group of people we meet with regularly is the most we ever need to defend—and often we don't even need to defend that.

To someone who says, "Church is boring", our first response should be (as always), "What do you mean by that?" If it turns out that it really is our public meetings they are commenting on, perhaps the only response needed is, "That's not my experience"—and then get back to real gospel issues.

One of the ways of sharing the gospel with people is by inviting them to church (in particular, inviting them to gospel meetings at our local church). For this sort of invitation to be helpful we almost certainly need to build a relationship first. Once they've been to our home, shared a meal with us and met some of our Christian friends, then old experiences of 'church' are likely to be less of a barrier.

On the other hand, to someone who says, "Church is awful" and who explains, in response to your standard "What do you mean by that?" question, that they are thinking of the public utterances or actions of certain denominations or denominational leaders, there is no real need to disagree or to defend such utterances or actions. Since our focus is the gospel, the most helpful thing to say is often going to be, "Yes, but what do you think about Jesus?"

As with 'religion', the goal is to quarantine 'church' so that it doesn't become a barrier to talking about who Jesus is and why he came.

Suffering

There are several different groups of people who are likely to raise questions about suffering.

First, there are those who are in the midst of suffering at the time they ask. Such people probably don't need theological explanations so much as sympathy and support. There are no biblical answers to questions about why these particular horrible things have happened to these particular people at this time. And speculation is not helpful.

A very wise pastor once said to me that a number of times over the years he's had people turn up at his church because their life had hit the skids (they'd been diagnosed with cancer, one of the kids had turned to drugs, the marriage had broken up, the career and income had fallen in a heap, etc.). Basically, they'd turned up for help, and to try to make sense of life. But, he added, he's never had anyone come to church saying, "Everything is going wonderfully well in my life and I wanted to find Someone to thank".

The grim truth is that when people are coping with life and all is going swimmingly, they are likely to feel that they don't need God. That, at least in part, is what Jesus means about rich men getting into heaven being like getting an elephant through a letterbox (or was it a camel through the eye of a needle?). Health and wealth convince most people that they don't need God. Grief can cause them to ask questions.

This is certainly not something to say to people who are suffering, but it is something to bear in mind while trying to help them. What is happening may be God at work in their lives. We work for the God who is working in them.

Hence, we should listen—patiently and sympathetically. We should provide as much practical help and assistance as we can. And if they get to a point when they do want to listen to answers, perhaps the first thing to explain is that God understands about suffering because God has suffered.

One of the most shallow and unhelpful things anyone can say to a sufferer is: "Oh, I know what you must be going through". No, you don't. Only the person going through it knows what it's really like. But God knows— not only because God is God and knows everything, but also because God has been through it before.

There is no suffering we can go through in this world that God has not already gone through. Is it physical pain? God has had six-inch iron spikes driven through his hands and feet to nail him to a wooden cross. Have you been betrayed and deserted? God the Son (Jesus Christ) was betrayed and deserted by his friends and followers. Have you suffered injustice? Jesus was put through a mockery of a trial and unjustly condemned to death. Have you seen a loved one die? God the Father has watched his own dearly beloved Son die an agonizing death on the cross.

God is the suffering God. He (and he alone) can fully understand and sympathize with a sufferer. God can understand and sympathize better than any human being on earth. The God to whom we can encourage people to take their questions and their pain is the suffering God.

Second, sometimes the question of suffering is raised by someone who has just thought of it as a knock-down argument against Christianity. This is the 15-year-old's triumphant discovery of a fool-proof argument against Christianity which, they seem to assume, no-one has ever thought of before.

Perhaps all that needs to be said to this person is that they themselves must explain how Christians—intelligent, thoughtful Christians—can suffer and still believe in a loving and powerful God. Christians have babies that die too. And yet they are still Christians. Is he (it's nearly always a 'he') suggesting that such Christians are all idiots? Or do Christians see something that he's missing?

This person may also be helped by the arguments that we use to respond to the third group.

These are people who are genuinely troubled by the problem of suffering. In my experience the issue arises not because they are suffering personally, but because of suffering that has been reported to them. They see the reports on television, they are deeply troubled by them, and they are worried that the world is out of control. Where, they ask, is the benevolent God who should prevent these things? Why did they happen?

They are exactly like a group of questioners who once approached Jesus with this concern. And the response of Jesus was shocking. He didn't say what you or I would be inclined to say in similar circumstances:

> There were some present at that very time who told
> him about the Galileans whose blood Pilate had
> mingled with their sacrifices. And he answered them,
> "Do you think that these Galileans were worse sinners
> than all the other Galileans, because they suffered in
> this way? No, I tell you; but unless you repent, you
> will all likewise perish. Or those eighteen on whom
> the tower in Siloam fell and killed them: do you think

that they were worse offenders than all the others who lived in Jerusalem? No, I tell you; but unless you repent, you will all likewise perish." (Luke 13:1-5)

Worried about the suffering in the world? Then repent. How can we translate this into something useful we can say when we are challenged in this way today?

It seems to me that the point here is that suffering doesn't happen because people deserve it (or because they're particularly unlucky, or something of that sort). Rather, suffering is part of the pattern of this world. Suffering happens because of where we live. We live on a planet in rebellion against God. We live in a world that has rejected God's rule. Our rebellion has corrupted every aspect of life in this world.

Ultimately, it is step two in our gospel outline ('sin') that explains suffering. So when suffering is reported to us, this should alert us to the fact that something is wrong with this world.

Complaining that life in this world hurts is like a man who lives on the equator complaining that it's hot. The answer in both cases is: "It's because of where you live".

This explanation can then lead us into explaining the six points of *Two Ways to Live*. Furthermore, Jesus says that the way to deal with suffering is to repent—to respond to the gospel challenge. So, how does this help? Is this a practical proposal? Coming from our all-wise saviour, we can be sure it is.

Repenting (responding to the challenge of the gospel)

deals with suffering in the following practical ways.

Firstly, it guarantees that suffering will end. At death (or at the second coming of Jesus, whichever happens first), suffering ends for the Christian. There is a line drawn in the sands of time beyond which suffering ends forever for those adopted into God's family: "He will wipe away every tear from their eyes, and death shall be no more, neither shall there be mourning nor crying nor pain anymore ..." (Rev 21:4). And knowing that the pain will end is powerful knowledge. You can bear the root-canal therapy because you know the dentist has another appointment in half an hour. But suffering ends only for believers. For unbelievers, death means an eternity of suffering: an eternity of angry, bitter isolation from God and from all that is worthwhile. In other words, Christians simply have to put up with this world. This is as bad as it ever gets for us. Unbelievers, however, have to enjoy this world—this is as good as it ever gets for them.

Secondly, repenting also means that suffering ceases to be meaningless. For the believer, constantly held in the hands of the powerful, loving, sovereign God, any suffering that God allows us to endure is part of his sovereign plan for our lives. What role it plays we cannot know. But we can know that, for Christians, this world is God's gymnasium making souls fit for his heaven: "For the Lord disciplines the one he loves, and chastises every son whom he receives. It is for discipline that you have to endure. God is treating you as sons. For what son is there whom his father does not discipline?" (Heb 12:6-7).

But pain and suffering are utterly meaningless for the unbeliever. They just happen. They are just part of living in this fallen, corrupt world.

Thirdly, when we turn to God he gives us each other. Christians do not stand alone; we stand together. The worst suffering is suffering alone. The prayers, the sympathy, the company and the practical support of fellow Christians can be powerful.

Fourthly, when we repent God gives us himself. In ways that may be beyond mere words to explain, Christ lives in us (if we are believing, born again Christians) giving us a strength and a comfort that we would not have expected, and could not account for in any other way, except that it is Christ at work in our lives.

In these ways, becoming a Christian deals practically with suffering. That's why Jesus' direction to those concerned about suffering ("Repent!") is really the best response that can be given.

In the face of questions about suffering, often the best defence of the gospel is simply to explain the gospel— which alone makes sense of the world we live in.

Truth

We supposedly live in something called the 'post-modern' age in which truth no longer exists. All truth, we are told, is relative. What is true for you is not necessarily true for me.

There is a degree of illusion here. So-called 'post-modernism' is an intellectual game that nobody lives out.

In fact, it is impossible to live as if there were no truth. People who are supposedly postmodern relativists still get angry over government policy. Why? If their frame of reference were genuine then they could say that for them, America never invaded Iraq. That's true for you and for *The Washington Post*, but it's not true for them.

In that sense, postmodern relativism does not need to be taken very seriously.

If someone claims to be a genuine postmodern relativist, ask them whether they'd like to fly with a postmodern relativist pilot—one who refuses to talk to air traffic control because "what's true for them is not true for him".

People who play the pseudo-intellectual game of postmodern relativism still cross the road when the traffic is clear. They don't try to cross in front of a speeding bus on the grounds that the notion of the bus being on the road is "not true for them".

And what is the case in the factual realm is also the case in the moral realm. I was once having a debate with a colleague who responded to every suggestion that there are moral standards that could be breached by saying, "It's all relative. It's all personal. What's right for you is right for you. You can't impose it on anyone else. They have to do what is right for them."

The response to this is to ask about, for instance, the Nazi death camps of World War II. When the guards at Auschwitz gassed innocent Jewish men, women and children, did the guards' belief that it was right make it right? Or are we right to condemn such behaviour as immoral?

On Sunday, 28 April 1996, the historic site of Port Arthur in Tasmania was crowded with tourists. At 1:30pm, a young man named Martin Bryant entered the Broad Arrow Cafe, pulled a high-powered rifle from a tennis bag he was carrying, and began shooting randomly at both adults and children.

Bryant then moved outside to the car park, shooting at, and setting fire to, several cars. Moving up the road he shot randomly at people as they arrived at the toll booth.

His next stop was the Fox and Hounds Hotel. He shot several people before moving further up the road to Seascape Lodge, where he killed all the occupants. He shot at helicopters taking his victims to hospital, and exchanged fire with police before he was finally captured.

In the end 35 people were dead and 20 wounded—the world's worst massacre by a lone gunman.

If this behaviour was right in Martin Bryant's eyes, does that make it right? The fact that we condemn such behaviour makes it clear that there is such a thing as an objective moral standard. We can argue about what such a standard is (where the line should be drawn), but not about the existence of such a standard.

There is objective, unchanging truth—both of a factual nature and of a moral nature. Most people, I suspect, believe this to be the case. If they claim otherwise, they are usually playing games and need to be brought back to earth.

In factual terms, the eight times table is true today,

just as it was true a thousand years ago. Likewise, the eight times table is true on this planet, on the moon, and on Mars.

The real question is not, "Is anything true?" That question is settled. There really are factual truths. Norway is a not a province of Canada. Paris is not the capital city of New Zealand. We know these to be facts, and many other things as well. The real question is: "Is biblical Christianity true?"

The answer to that depends upon the reliability of the Bible. How do we know that the Bible is true? Well, how do we know that anything is true? What are the usual tests of truth claims?

First, there's the test of observation. Does what we observe fit with what we read? This is traditionally called the 'correspondence' test: does what we read correspond with what we observe?

In the case of the Bible the answer is a resounding "Yes!" For instance, the more work done by historians and archaeologists, the more supporting observations there are for the truth of the Bible's historical claims.[2]

Then there's the test of consistency. Are the truth claims consistent? Or are there built-in contradictions? This is traditionally called the 'coherence' test: do all of the claims and assertions we read in the Bible fit together consistently, without contradiction?

---

[2]   For more on this question, see the useful book by Paul Barnett, *Is the New Testament History?*, rev. edn, Aquila, Sydney, 2003.

And once again the answer is a resounding "Yes!" The Bible tells a single, coherent, consistent story from beginning to end. The Bible is a collection of 66 documents written by some 40 authors, over more than a thousand years—and yet it has a single plot line, and tells a single story, focusing on a single theme. That is pretty remarkable. In fact, it's evidence that all 40 human authors were actually 'co-authors' inspired by the Bible's true author: God.[3]

We need, in our conversations with unbelievers, to avoid playing the mind games of so-called 'postmodern relativists'. In daily life, in the real world, everyone lives as if there is such a thing as truth. That daily reality is the real meaning of the word 'truth'. Christianity passes those real-world truth tests with flying colours.

THE FOCUS IN THIS CHAPTER has been on dealing with possible barriers raised by non-gospel issues. In particular we have focused on how we negotiate the potential barriers of religion, church, suffering and truth.

As always, we will do best at getting around such

---

[3]   If you'd like to know more about this, check out *Gospel and Kingdom: A Christian Interpretation of the Old Testament* (Paternoster, Carlisle, UK, 1994) by Graeme Goldsworthy. This is a good place to start looking at the single, consistent plot line of the Bible.

barriers and back to the gospel by listening closely and carefully, and by responding with gentleness and respect.

In some cases we may not have immediate answers. In those cases, we should promise to do some research and come back with answers. And if we make that promise then we must treat people with respect, and do what we undertake. This, too, is an essential part of our defence of the gospel.

Chapter 9

WHO ARE YOU TALKING TO?

Finally, NOT EVERYONE TO WHOM you are 'giving answers' and 'making a defence' will be the same. And different people can be helped in different ways. In this last chapter I briefly want to consider different types of unbelievers you might encounter.[1]

1. The hostile

There is a good deal of open hostility to Jesus and to the Bible these days. Some people who take a thoroughly

---

[1]   This list of seven types of unbelievers comes from an old (and now out of print) book called *Personal Work* by Percy O. Ruoff. A current book that I can recommend is *Biblical Strategies for Witness* by Dr Peter Masters (Wakeman Trust, London, 1994)—it classifies unbelievers under four headings and looks at how Jesus handled each of these four types.

materialistic point of view (which they think of as being 'scientific') will gleefully seize any opportunity to mock belief in the Bible and commitment to Jesus.

At a purely intellectual level, such people often have closed minds and are not open to logical argument. However, if behind the sneers and hostility there is any glimmer of genuine intellectual curiosity about Christianity, then there are arguments and evidence that can help.

For instance, such people believe or assume that everything is inside the 'materialistic box'. I picture this as a box labelled 'matter and energy'—which these people insist contains all there is. There is nothing, they say, outside the box. So it might be worth pointing out that the 'materialistic box' simply **can't** contain everything, nor can it explain everything that demands explanation.

Take a poem, for instance. If it is analyzed materialistically, it consists of ink and paper. But the most minute examination of this will, in fact, miss the actual poem—the real thing itself. The poem is actually something else, something non-material that exists in a non-material realm of creativity, imagination, spirit, the mind, the human soul ... or whatever label you want to use.

There are those things with which we are familiar, that cannot be fully explained physically. They exist in a realm beyond the physical. It was to account for such things that Aristotle coined the word 'metaphysics' (literally, "after physics").

If science explained everything physical about

human life and the universe we live in, there would still be an unexplained residue left over. A great painting is not just paint dabs on canvas. A great piece of music is not just sound vibrations in the air. There is clearly something else going on at another level beyond the merely physical.

Further, the world view of such people cannot adequately account for morality. All materialists deny this, but it remains true. The argument with which C. S. Lewis begins his book *Mere Christianity* might help at this point. He calls this argument "Right and wrong as a clue to the meaning of the universe". If you read those chapters,[2] you could summarize them in a conversation. Or you could simply lend or give a copy of *Mere Christianity*.

Very briefly, Lewis points out that everyone is aware of a moral law. We all appeal to some standard of behaviour—for instance, when we argue about what is the right thing to do. We might not agree on what the standard is, but we all acknowledge that there is a standard. That standard, that moral law, can only be explained by the existence of a moral law-giver—namely, God. There is, of course, a great deal more to the argument, and for that you should consult *Mere Christianity*.

Finally, such hostility often comes from a deep desire on the part of the hostile person for God not to exist. And this, in turn, can spring from a desire not to be bound by moral or ethical commitments. If God exists, and

---

[2] C. S. Lewis, op. cit., Book I, chapters 1-5.

morality has an eternal foundation, then this person cannot have a series of casual affairs, or steal from the boss, or whatever. We'll consider such people—the immoral—later in this chapter.

With the aggressive atheist, the openly and mockingly hostile person, sometimes all that can be done is to pray for that person, to live Christianly in front of them, and to respond to their jibes gently and respectfully by standing firm on intelligent, well-informed belief in Jesus and the Bible.

2. The philosophically-minded

It is important with philosophically-minded people not to present Christianity as a competing philosophy among a world of philosophies. We live in an age when people like to think of different philosophies and world views as a smorgasbord from which they can pick and choose. If an Eastern philosophy appeals to them, they will pick that. If something more stoic or more hedonistic appeals, they will pick that. If they've done some philosophy at university, they may have a 'quilt-like' world view made up of different philosophical bits and pieces.

There are two points that can be helpful here.

The first is that all philosophies and world views are human inventions—human speculations. Some are extremely clever, others less so. Some have the dignity of being extremely ancient, others are more modern inventions. But all can be traced back to a human source—sometimes, as in Buddhism or Scientology, to a single human source. In other cases, as in Hinduism or Existentialism, it is a way of thinking and believing that developed among numbers of thinkers over time. But all are of human origin.

The claim Christians make is that we didn't make it up. The challenge to such people is this: if there really is a creator God who stands behind the universe, and if such a God chose to communicate with human beings, what would the message look like? Our answer is that the message would look like Jesus. He is not another example of humans reaching up to God; rather, Jesus is God reaching down to us. He is God's last word, God's complete message, to humanity. We ignore him at our peril.

The second point ties in with this first point. We can direct people to the character of Jesus. We can point to his wisdom, his insight, his authority, his dignity and his compassion. Then we can point out that this remarkable person also claimed to be God. That is the real challenge the philosophically-minded dabbler needs to face.

3. The tolerant

Tolerance is a much misunderstood concept in the modern world. The verb 'to tolerate' came into the English language in the 16th century from a Latin source word, and means 'to bear with' or 'to put up with'.

So the original meaning of 'tolerance' was to bear with people, to put up with them, to endure them. Today it is assumed that 'tolerance' means to agree with people. If you don't agree with people, it's now assumed that you are being intolerant.

The Christian has to be prepared to insist that real tolerance says something different. Real tolerance says, "I don't agree with you—I think you're wrong—and yet even so, I will passionately defend your right to be wrong. I don't believe different views should be censored, and I want to hear what you have to say. But I also believe that I have a right to explain what I believe. I reject all censorship of ideas and the use of force to suppress debate, and I believe passionately in the right we have to try to persuade each other. In all this I remain your friend."

That is true tolerance.

The other muddled thinking about what tolerance is comes from the idea that all religions are really much the same: "All roads are winding up the same mountain. It's just that each is taking a different path." This kind of thinking is a reflection not of tolerance but of ignorance.

The reality is that all religions are radically different and many are irreconcilable with the others, often at a very basic level.

For instance, take the issue of death. Here are three competing views: (a) at death, we are all snuffed out and have no further existence; (b) at death, we are all reincarnated and return to life on earth in a different body; and (c) at death, we face judgement followed by eternal rewards or punishment. Those three views are fundamentally incompatible. If any one is true, then the other two must be false. To pretend that all three can somehow simultaneously be true is not tolerant. It is ignorant.

On the subject of this so-called modern 'tolerance',

the Christian can say two things. Firstly, as we've just pointed out, all religions do not agree and do not all say the same thing. Secondly, as we've argued in the previous chapter, Christianity is not a religion.

4. The indifferent

The hardest people to reach with the gospel are those who simply don't care. They are unconcerned about spiritual matters.

Such people are simply very short-sighted. They are looking down at their feet, not up at the horizon. They are preoccupied with the immediate. For some, it is leisure and pleasure that fills their time and their thinking. For others, it is career. For yet others, it is money and what it will buy. They are not interested in the bigger picture of the meaning and purpose of life.

Some people in this category think Christians are far too serious and earnest, and the whole point of life is to have fun. It may well be the case that such people won't be open to hearing the gospel until the fun runs out, and life gets tough for them.

Others in this group are convinced that life is about material success: "Whoever has the most toys when he dies, wins!" This, of course, is not true. Whoever has the most toys when he dies, still dies. With these people it may be the case that they are not open to the gospel until they have reached their goals and found not satisfaction but emptiness.

With all truly indifferent people it is possible to say

that there are two reasons why everyone should examine the claims of Jesus Christ. First: you will die. Second: you don't know when. Not acting now to investigate is like having no money in the bank, no car insurance, and driving in heavy traffic at high speed.

But even confronting an indifferent person so directly will not always generate interest. Death is often dismissed by such people as something to be worried about "later". Patience, and real friendship, and the planting of small 'seed' thoughts can sometimes be the only option.

5. The ignorant

We live in a world that, by and large, hasn't the faintest idea of what the Christian gospel is. Most of the people I meet seem to think that Christianity is about going to church, with its attendant ceremonies and rules. They think that what Jesus taught was all about being good.

We are dealing today with second- and third-generation pagans. There was a time when even non-churchgoers sent their children to Sunday School. But that was two generations ago. It doesn't happen nearly so much today, and the result is widespread ignorance.

The idea that the Bible consists of two testaments is news to many people today. For many, Matthew, Mark, Luke and John are just common boys' names—not the names of the four Gospel writers. If they open a Bible, almost the first thing they have to understand is that the big numbers are chapters and the little numbers are verses.

What is needed for the ignorant is a basic, simple, clear explanation of the gospel, such as the six points of *Two Ways to Live*. If they begin to show some interest—perhaps in response to remarks you've made in passing, or simply because they are intrigued that one of their friends is that weird thing, 'a Christian'—then the best thing you can do is to say, "I've been learning a way to explain what Christians believe; can I practise on you?" If they say, "Yes", take them through the six points of the *Two Ways to Live* gospel outline.

Nothing can deal with ignorance except information.

6. The religious

These are people for whom religion is like an insurance policy. If they have done the right things, or been 'done' by the right denomination, they think they have taken out their insurance policy with God and will be okay.

Some may be Roman Catholics; others may be Mormons or Scientologists or Jehovah's Witnesses or may belong to one of the Eastern religions. If you have a friend in such a category, it can be helpful to read a book that explains their religious beliefs from a Christian perspective. This will help you to understand their jargon, and the categories in which they think—and that is part of treating them with respect.

At the risk of lumping a lot of different religious beliefs together, it seems to me that often such religious people are not interested in submitting to God but in manipulating God.

They seem to think of God as what I call 'the great Coca Cola machine in the sky'. They put in their 'coin'. This 'coin' may be church attendance, or being baptized and confirmed, or confessing and receiving mass, or prayer, or having some sort of spiritual experience, or being a nice, upright citizen. In response, out pops what they have paid for—not a can of Coke but a ticket to heaven.

In the end, what such people really need to see is the power and necessity of the death of Jesus Christ on the cross. The best way to make this clear can be to say, "May I explain to you what I believe?"—and take them through the six steps of the *Two Ways to Live* gospel outline. Against the background of that outline, you can then leave them firstly with the necessity of the death and resurrection of Jesus, and secondly with the absolute assurance of salvation found in Jesus.

This second point is important because these variously religious people very often have no sense of certainty or assurance of their eternal spiritual destiny. The gospel makes it clear that such certainty is possible.

And, of course, with such people the remarks made in the previous chapter under the heading of 'Religion' may well be helpful.

7. The immoral

A friend of mine was once sharing the gospel with a business executive. After some discussion the executive finally said, "But I'd have to change the way I live, wouldn't I?" This man was notoriously, and fairly openly, having an affair with his secretary. My friend responded, "Yes, you would". The executive immediately lost all interest.

Many of the reasons people give for rejecting Jesus and the Bible are, in reality, excuses. What they are really avoiding is giving up their sin. "The light has come into the world, and people loved the darkness rather than the light because their deeds were evil" (John 3:19).

Many years ago John Bunyan addressed such people by saying, "Will you keep your sin and go to hell, or will you give up your sin and go to heaven?" Such a direct approach is probably a bit strong for one-to-one conversation, but the point is well made. The truth is that what is gained is far greater than what is lost when people give up the 'pleasures' of immorality.

Christianity—personally following Jesus Christ—is not just the best way to die, it is also the best way to live. The real joys, and the real security, of the Christian life—even in this fallen, corrupt world—far outweigh the fleeting pleasures of self-indulgence.

Sometimes these individuals will defend their immoral behaviour by saying something like, "God wants me to be happy". The answer is: "No, God doesn't want you to be happy; he wants you to be holy. If you have to become unhappy to be holy, then God will make you unhappy." God's aim is that human beings become more like Jesus Christ, not more like King Herod with his self-indulgent lifestyle.

Perhaps the best thing that can be done to persuade people in this category to take an interest in the gospel is for them to meet, and socialize with, your Christian friends. Let them catch a glimpse of what living the Christian life is really like, and they just might think again.

Chapter 10

CONCLUSION

Oᴜʀ ɢᴏᴀʟ ɪs ᴛʜᴀᴛ ᴏᴜʀ ꜰʀɪᴇɴᴅs, our relatives, our colleagues, will hear the gospel of Jesus Christ—for that is the power that can change their lives, and change them for good: "For I am not ashamed of the gospel, for it is the power of God for salvation to everyone who believes ..." (Rom 1:16).

This is the gospel we are called upon to defend in all our relationships and conversations. If our friends want to sneer at our denomination, let them. Our denomination cannot save them. But the gospel of Jesus Christ can.

If they want to condemn something they call 'religion', or more specifically 'the Christian religion', because of horror stories in the media, then we don't need to get into a passionate debate with them. We need to get them back to thinking about who Jesus is and why he came.

What we need is commitment to real friendships, and to being real friends. You can sometimes be a friend with someone and pray for them for years before they show an interest in the gospel.

There is a story told about George Müller, the great 19th-century prayer warrior and founder of Christian orphanages. He had two lifelong non-Christian friends. He prayed for them, and talked to them about Christian things, for the whole of his life. One of these men became a Christian shortly before Müller died at the age of 93. The other man became a Christian after Müller died.

If we are to do any worthwhile work for the gospel of Jesus Christ, we need real friendships with unbelievers—friendships that we don't give up on. And in the context of those friendships we must be faithful to God's command in 1 Peter 3:15 to be ready, to be prepared, so that when we are asked gospel questions we will have something to say that will point towards the grace of God in Jesus Christ.

Appendix

DISCUSSION GUIDE

THE QUESTIONS THAT FOLLOW are designed to help you discuss the content of *Defending the Gospel* with others—your spouse, or a friend, or the small group you meet with at church. Use these questions as a way of talking back over the content of each chapter, and encouraging each other to put God's word into practice.

Chapter 1: Defending, answering and giving reasons

1. Read 1 Peter 3:15-16. How are you currently responding to this command of Scripture?
2. What steps does the chapter recommend we take?
3. Read Colossians 4:2-6. In what situations do you have opportunities to answer graciously?

Chapter 2: Defending God

1. Do you think it is worth trying to prove the existence of God? Why or why not? (Cf. Rom 1:18-20; Ps 19:1-6.)
2. "Science argues process, not purpose." Put this idea in your own words—as you might explain it to a friend.
3. Role-play or talk through a discussion with someone who doesn't believe in the existence of God. How might you lead the conversation in a useful direction—for example, to talking about Jesus? If discussing in a group, try different approaches.
4. How would you respond to someone who thought that God wouldn't be interested in them?

Chapter 3: Defending sin

1. Look at Romans 1:18-25, 3:10-12; Mark 7:20-22; 1 John 3:4, and 1 John 2:8-11. What different definitions of sin can you come up with?
2. How are these definitions consistent with each other?
3. "I'm not as bad as the Bible says I am." How would you answer the person who says this?

Chapter 4: Defending judgement

1. Summarize some of the things that Jesus says about judgement in the following passages from the Gospels: Mark 9:43-48; Matt 5:22 and 27-30, 7:23, 8:12, 10:28, 13:40-42, 18:8-9, 25:30-46; Luke 16:24. What is judgement like in these passages? What is the basis for judgement? (Check from the context of the verses quoted.)
2. What would you say to someone who doesn't believe that judgement is fair?
3. "The Old Testament is all about judgement, but the New Testament and Jesus are all about love." How would you respond to this statement?

Chapter 5: Defending Jesus

1. How are the following passages evidence that Jesus thought he was God: Mark 2:3-12; John 8:39-59?
2. How would you respond to someone who believed that Jesus was a wise teacher but no more than that?
3. Why did Jesus have to die? Refer to Mark 10:45; Rom 3:25-26, 5:6-8; 1 Pet 3:18; 1 John 3:8.

Chapter 6: Defending the resurrection

1. Summarize as many arguments against Jesus' bodily resurrection as you can think of. How would you answer them from the Bible?
2. Look at Acts 2:17-36 and Acts 17:29-34. According to these two passages, what does the resurrection 'prove'?
3. "You get old and sick, then you die, and that's the end of life and hope." How does the reality of the resurrection help answer this statement?

Chapter 7: Defending the challenge

1. How does the Bible answer the person who believes there are many ways to God (see John 14:6)?
2. How does the Bible help us to respond to someone who wants to delay responding (see Luke 12:13-21)?
3. How does the Bible help answer the person who asks, "What about those who have never heard about Jesus?" (see Rom 2:1-16)?

Chapter 8: Four big issues

Pick one or more of these four issues, and discuss how you would bring a discussion on one of these issues back to the gospel (look up any Bible passages mentioned in the chapter).

Chapter 9: Who are you talking to?

1. Can you think of people you know who are like the types of people mentioned in this chapter? Can you think of other types?

2. Do you think we should have different approaches to different people? Why or why not?

3. Read Romans 1:16-17 and Philippians 1:15-18.

   a. What does Paul reveal about his attitude to the message of the gospel?

   b. How does this help address question 2 above?

Matthias Media is a ministry team of like-minded, evangelical Christians working together to achieve a particular goal, as summarized in our mission statement:

> To serve our Lord Jesus Christ, and the growth of his gospel in the world, by producing and delivering high quality, Bible-based resources.

It was in 1988 that we first started pursuing this mission together, and in God's kindness we now have more than 250 different ministry resources being distributed all over the world. These resources range from Bible studies and books, through to training courses and audio sermons.

To find out more about our large range of very useful products, and to access samples and free downloads, visit our website:

www.matthiasmedia.com.au

How to buy our resources

1. Direct from us over the internet:
   – in the US: www.matthiasmedia.com
   – in Australia and the rest of the world: www.matthiasmedia.com.au

2. Direct from us by phone:
   – in the US: 1 866 407 4530
   – in Australia: 1800 814 360 (Sydney: 9663 1478)
   – international: +61-2-9663-1478

3. Through a range of outlets in various parts of the world. Visit **www.matthiasmedia.com.au/international.php** for details about recommended retailers in your part of the world, including www.thegoodbook.co.uk in the United Kingdom.

4. Trade enquiries can be addressed to:
   – in the US: sales@matthiasmedia.com
   – in the UK: sales@ivpbooks.com
   – in Australia and the rest of the world: sales@matthiasmedia.com.au

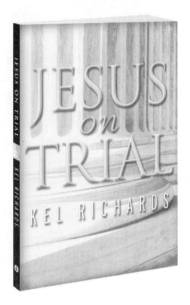

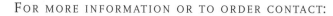

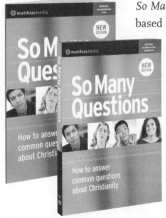